Collected Works Volume Eight

The Poems

Nigel Pearce

chipmunkapublishing
the mental health publisher

All rights reserved, no part of this publication may be reproduced by any means, electronic, mechanical photocopying, documentary, film or in any other format without prior written permission of the publisher.

>Published by
>Chipmunkapublishing
>United Kingdom

http://www.chipmunkapublishing.com

Copyright © 2023 Nigel Pearce

The Poems.

> You ask me why I spend my life writing?
> […] I write only because/ There is
> a voice within me/ That will not be still

- Sylvia. Plath, Letters Home: Correspondence (2010). Faber & Faber

Those Mugwumps and a Chindit.

Seemed a Mugwump sprung like a spring and scampered into a convoluted boy,
They carried corrosive waste, a health hazard, those lizardspenetrated his mind,
Then shook the hand of a psychiatrist who performed crazed. lobotomies at night,

A millstone had crushed the child poet's mind into chaff, the Mugwumps had bred,
They created translucent mosquitoes, blood-sucking, brain-melting ones who glare,
These Mugwumps became bloated and hungry full or heroin just as Burroughs' worms.

His father had been a Benzedrine-driven guerrilla because the Chindits did not rest,
He tried to gouge out those leaches
 from his arms as his father had done in Burma;
Crazy at times I lie in that coffin prepared by the Chindit
 and write that curled poetry.

Note:
In the William Burroughs novel Naked Lunch, which follows the narration of a junkie, William Lee, Mugwumps are a predatory, alien species. "On stools covered in white satin sit naked Mugwumps sucking translucent, coloured syrup through alabaster straws," Burroughs wrote. "Mugwumps have no liver and nourish themselves exclusively on sweets. Thin, purple-blue lips cover

a razor-sharp beak of black bone with which they frequently tear each other to shreds in fights over clients."

Bleach Bath: A poem employing T.S. Eliot's 'objective-correlative.'
A set of objects, a situation, a chain of events shall be the formula of that particular emotion.
         Hamlet and His Problems. T.S. Eliot. 1921. The Sacred Wood ...

This bath was just a variation on a theme,
The big black boot and the clenched fist,
 Revolutionaries expect this, even us kids,
But their repertoire in their house of Care.

A welcome was written numerically '666.'
On that superintendent's forehead, S.S,
For an intense hour, you could cut the air,
A rat arrived; he locked me in a bathroom.

'You're a good boy undress',
He had emptied some bleach into a bath,
About four inches slightly diluted, 'get in,'
He just drawls; 'All communists are dirty',

Never saw him again; he was brought in
To teach me a lesson and soften me up,

But it failed.

The incident still smarts and is unforgiven,
The red reaper will avenge these crimes,
Our Nemesis will flush rats out of sewers,
There is nowhere to hide from class justice.

Ian (R.I.P.): a documentary poem.

For him, I still can weep hot tears,

Ian was a fresher from Cambridge,
His mistake was to take an acid tab,
But he did not then soar to Heaven
Or descend into the fierce, fiery pit.

No, Ian's giant brain was scrambled,
They brought him in to the hospital,
Wild wide eyes, but blessedly calm,
Will you sit with him: 'yes, of course.'

That crazy man, Ian, showed me how
To solve a puzzle, the cosmic enigma,
A pack of cards Ian placed randomly,
Every day in a different configuration.

But Ian began rebalancing his scales,
Singing those Leonard Cohen songs,
A guitar strummed, if slightly off-key,
We loved it, not noticing his repertoire,

So sad songs Ian sung, smile beguiled,
but the doctors discharged him too early,
Frequently he housed me as an orphan,
After dad ejaculated me as 'a damn red'.

We were two roamers of the labyrinth,
Our wings had melted, contorted gladly.
One dark dawn slapped him, he hung,
But Ian had left no note of explanation.

The Inferno and Beyond.

(a sequence of 'voices' from Council Care, psychiatry, and the counterculture).

      Refuse to be an accomplice Don't lie - don't keep your eyes shut.
-     Simone Weil in Zaretsky, Robert (2021) The Subversive Simone Weil: A Life in Five Ideas. p, 39.

The Inferno and Beyond.

Introductory Summary.

My inspiration was derived from a diversity of poets: Sappho, Dante, Milton, William Wordsworth, William Carlos Williams, Brecht, Allen Ginsburg, Sylvia Plath, James Wright and others. Wordsworth importantly embraced 'the real language of men' Preface to Lyrical Ballads and an introspective turn in The Prelude. The concomitant rupture of Modernism in the early poetry of T.S. Eliot and Ezra Pound is equally significant. As was William Carlos Williams' response. His use of juxtaposing different types of text impacted my writing. While the 'confessional verse' of especially Sylvia Plath is a significant influence. I also agree with William Burroughs: In my writing, I am acting as a map maker, an explorer of psychic areas, a cosmonaut of inner space, and I see no point in exploring areas that have already been thoroughly surveyed.
- William Burroughs in Chad Weidner (2016) The Green Ghost: William Burroughs and the Ecological Mind, p.7.

Finally, I also used closed forms in recognition of the impact of New Formalism. My vision is multitudinous as it befits one who has mental ill-health. This collection gives 'voice' to those who experienced Council 'Care', the psychiatric system and counterculture. I followed Simone Weil's advice, kept my eyes open, and observed.

In reading T. S. Eliot's (1953) The Three Voices of Poetry.

In a lecture delivered in 1953, "The Three Voices of Poetry", T. S. Eliot said that "dramatic monologue cannot create a character". As his title implies, Eliot distinguishes between three voices of poetry. The first voice is that "of the poet talking to himself-or to nobody", and the second voice is that "of the poet addressing an audience", and the third "is the voice of the poet when he attempts to create a dramatic character speaking in verse".

Do I write poems for the daughters and sons of Moloch? Do I scribe verse for a leap in trade union consciousness? Do I write in several voices, as Eliot had argued in 1953?

One more for the men who flagellate alone, boozed, Another for a woman who told me of her fisted abuse, Lines for junk sick, and mad youths who will die soon.

Some more for the good and bad psychiatrists
Who are caring for cash?
Yet do they spend it all on their lewd midnight bash

Awash with a little more than drinky poos, yes, it is coke,
Gives that sparkle, stare, and glare; the doctor still smells of the night before, yet I guess that there was no time to

CHANGE.

So, dish out the sedatives and do not forget to take one

YOURSELF.

A Shakespearian Sonnet to Eleanor Marx. 1855 - 1898.

Tussy, so you could only be his incarnation,
The heights and depths of heaving workers,
A fatal flaw is a scar, a martyr's inclination,
Sigh and feel; never be like leaden bankers.
A Polish, Jewish, Irishwoman girl of the light,
Organized the women and girls match strike,
Will Thorn, who you taught to read and write,
A comrade of William Morris (he did not fight).

You translated Ibsen for the benighted masses,
Madame Bovary with that misogynist Aveling,
He was death in life, a cobra biting your riches,
So, strike he did quite like a snake with a sting.
Your prussic acid and chloroform made dead,
Your blood has stained our flag a deeper red.

Mother (Maxim Gorky) 1.
An Ars Poetica study.
My mum had not perused the Gorky,
Or marched the streets on May Day,
Did not know of his bright Red Flame;
she was an actress in the play of ivy.

My mother had not moved into the fray;
the path I took was like a dawn sunrise.
But, mum danced with veils and masks
And deceived many who twirled blind.

I read Mother at the Party Congress
The comrades brought food, coffee,
Kind folk, but I sat alone in a canteen,
And fell in love with this boxed novel.

Then hoped that some red epiphany
Would impact upon my sad mother,
She, a woman of the night in a day,
Who performed the bourgeois rituals,

While we made Molotov Cocktails,
In Derry, Handsworth, and Brixton,
The vanguardists without mothers,
She lived in a closed, tightened net.

1 https://www.marxists.org/archive/gorky-maxim/1906/mother/index.htm

My mum had been making suicidal suggestions
to me since I was seven.

Like Hugh MacDiarmid, my reading age was quite
advanced. When there was no suicide attempt: I
politely asked: 'Are you going to kill yourself,
mum.'
The chilly reply: 'I was just letting off steam.' I had
to grow up wildly, quickly upon fallow ground.
I understood as a child that she was entrapped in
a cage called the family; Mum was a free spirit
who should have lived in an artist's colony.

I would leave for the counterculture at age eleven,
fleeing what was a little more than a war zone; the
Fuhrer and Mater screamed at each other but with
a bellicose bellow against my ideas.

> Yet I loved her, and when the moon beckons,
> Dig with torn hands into her entombed heart.

Sonnet for my other lost (foster) family.

They did mistake a tear with Hegel's Idea, This bat flew with no eyes, no illusion,
I came into their world without that fear, With sounds at dusk, not any pollution. Then heat roared until your brain boils, Dad was a transmitter, like a Lukács, They had reaped their gains and spoils, Your brain had farrows, prepared a stash.

You were the type to make them look a twit, When the epoch did not collapse, a clown You moved into business; I almost had a fit, The tide had turned, but you had not a frown. The group would soon merely use your name; I thought that it was more than just a shame

Lines on Brigitte M', a leading member of the S.P.K (Socialist Patients' Collective).
A chill and steel grimace glares and stares From the steel goblet from which she sips; substitutions are easy in the class struggle; she didn't substitute emotions with zeros.

Replace the proletariat with a vanguard? Never replace authenticity with their shit; kill a revolutionist with a gun or tablets, Yet they will rise like your fear of death.

From this cup drunk Brigitte M, not the China tea-services of the oppressor, She smiled as that red wine of love Intoxicated her with a fantastic desire

To destroy daddy in every manifestation.

She was an incarnation, the realization, And beatification of our red insurrection;.
her gun shot lemon butterflies of love.

Daddy, Daddy, you bastard, I am through - Sylvia Plath, Daddy.

The Gym-Mat 'in Care.'
Holy, Holy the Fifth International […]
- Allen Ginsburg, Howl.

S.S, the superintendent did not like politicos, at least not red rebels in his Care institution; we were several boys and girls, the minority; his tricks are well known to his kind, to divide.

An Assessment Centre on a summer evening, He sunk beneath the line of decency as we Expected child-care officers arranged a bout, A gym mat boxing gloves, two of us refused.

They whipped the other children into a mob of jeers; we stood alone resolute for half an hour, Comrade Then said: 'I am sorry, I have to hit you', we danced. Sparring then a blow landed, blood is red.

Just as we were, so we shouted: 'Long live the Fifth International.'
They were mute, aptly abashed and will soon be smashed.

Ward 19 at Hollymoor Hospital, Birmingham, 1974.

Just about fourteen, and Fate had cracked The
bell, which had chimed a blunt o'clock, Discord in
my head for Ward 19 had a bed, And a comrade
detained in Care was sent.

A crazed creature kept hurtling at the walls; his
body had bounced off bruised and bled,
Again, again, this was not any game, I realised;
these were men; why was I a child confined?

I want to go back to the adolescent Unit, I plead,
Say that again, and you have another Largactil…
The last one, I swear, had almost killed me; it did.
No refuge on 19's on the T.V around 8.35 p.m.

The Mulberry Bush erupts as staff stand stare, But
Bedlam undulates just like the tidal ocean,
Skeleton staff rattled, and a church firebombed, A
burr of nurses and doctors maintained scales.

I was back in the Unit as most staff had returned,
There was a smell of fear, an atmosphere I noted.
Learnt names: Liam and Bernadette; Gerry
smiled.

Hannah on Ward 10 at Hollymoor Hospital, Birmingham, 1975.

Hannah, you do not and cannot stop the wailing; it has been weeks;
still, the tears flow in torrents; I am so sorry and would gladly sacrifice
 myself In your synagogue to wash, absent your stains
n orthodox Jewess, a jewel with mousy hair,
Something had snapped in Tel Aviv at age 19,
Went sky high and slept all the way to the U.K.,
The men are damned, used a nymphomaniac.

Their leering eyes would not see your mania,
Only what lust-dripping salivating lips desired;
 I saw the damage they had wreaked at fifteen,
It created a lifelong loathing of that type of man.

What befell Hannah would remain a mystery;
She floated away one sultry summer evening.
Family, suicide, or those demons of Mossad,
 I Never again saw Hannah with her mousy hair.

A poet becomes catatonic in a psychiatric hospital.

His body of dust is fleeing the squares of black to white, the black and white tiled corridors winding, with no end; H is smooth veil of tissue was torn cast into a river of sand.

Writing is transience as it is trapped in a house of mirrors. With the Dead, who kiss with burnt words like bubbling acid, It blistered his lips until poetry was left choked and silenced.

The remembrance of an attempt to abuse me in an asylum.

What a loon was Vic, the nurse; Nurse Goodall wore sharp suits,

He was bathing me, too ill to myself; I was out of the bath; talcum powder Kept going up and up my legs. 'If you try that on. I will put you through the bloody wall.'
He backs off, but two days later, alone in the male Common room. He grabs hippy hair and then pulls Me the room's width, saying, 'I'll show you what violence is.' It was my word against his status.
It would have been futile; Largactil jab awaited.

Like all victims of abuse had thought I was alone. After all, he had given me some Rupert Brooke; he was struck off and would be an early A.I.D.s casualty.

They let him return, but I was not sad when he died.

The House on the hill.

An ivy house on the hill for those with dreamy dreams,
Or said anonymous gods who strode in dirty white coats
Around the wards with even black and white tiled floors,
A nurse said, 'you are a no hoper' I was reading Sartre.

Tuesdays and Fridays, we were wired to the grid, E.C.T.
Routine rather than diagnosis, fancy rather than science.
My Child Care Order expired; they had to become careful.
The attitude was abruptly altered, no jabs or those shocks.

Metamorphosis: 'you are clever and creative', they say,
'Try the Open University in 1988', have degrees gained
Books published; a tempest of a voyage remains ahead,
Many did not survive; each death is etched on my heart.

I stand solitary, encapsulated by books, yet alive, writing.

Asylum.

A house on that hill had close manicured lawns,
Summer kissed lawns, but it burnt the patients,
The long stayers had old clothes that did not fit,
The staff just sat nodding into each other's eyes.

The psychiatrists whooshed around as Dervishes,
 until exhausted sunk whisky,
They were Father Confessors in this purgatory.
You had better give up all hope once admitted.

No one had anticipated the coming demolition,
It became a housing estate; many are homeless.

A priest realized God is dead and mourns.

A deep chasm of coldness is beating in this grinding Heart;
here, lovers' warmth had ridden like dawn,
He celebrated Mass, transubstantiation, and libation.

Now he is standing stunned in torn vestments
Night has enfolded his soul,
 the sacrificial Rite Of Winter, and frost has frozen into a river of ice.

Empty whisky bottles did say an awful lot more
 than he would have ever preached to his flock.

Hymn to the Mortality of the Nazarene.

The Void beckons like graves welcome the dead; Mary weaves barbed Threads of wire, dark mystery, to coronate her poet who moves forward, To glance into an infinity of broken glass, her eyes of smiles, circles of black, There were stains on a bed, but it was here she washed the blood from sheets; these tinges are bled in a cycle of betrayal and love, the Sunset and Sunrise.

He wipes the tears of mortality from his eyes and steps to look beyond the edge, A taunting precipice; he howled, 'Father, Abba, why did you let my corpse hang Among unclean men and these anemic women?' 'Mother, why did not your blood Mingle with the blood flowing from my wounds in my hands, in my feet, and side? You blessed the wisdom of fools in the shifting sand, that myopia of the deserts.'

This infant, the Lamb, is a man tuned into those pulsations of Alpha and Omega.

He leaps into the Void to dance with the eternal damned.

W. H. Auden visited us, patients, as a Christmas Treat.
The applause of literate nurses and pampered patients was deafening.

The great poet tended to the needy for a fee; he was not Christlike,
I wonder how much these people know about this celebrity poet.

I rise: 'Spain c:1936 is wiped clean from your repertoire because of ….
'Who is that inmate', snaps Auden, like a military Staff Sargent to infantry,
'That is one of our more challenging patients.' replies Staff Nurse, smirking,
"Why did you censor: 'the young poets exploding with necessary murder.'
And 'Yesterday, the song at sunset/ The adoration of the Madman/ But
today the struggle.'" 'I will not be heckled by a lunatic, that deluded nutter.'

A young doctor joins the melee: 'Mr. Auden, you wrote those lines although I understand since your conversion, they may indeed smart more than a little.'

'You are all deranged. Doctors and patients, keep your fantasies to yourself.'
'A first edition is a textual proof.'
'You cretinous idiots, take that.' A non-metaphorical pitcher of water is hurled
 across the hall. It hits the senior consultant, who is soaked.

A chime of cheers cascades from first the patients, a gaggle of giggles from those Student nurses and

then 'you seem a little overwrought from the Professor, a pill
would put that right.'
'Get away from me; I am leaving.'
"Not so rapidly, W.H. You seem agitated; could I venture in need of a little rest,
on Ward No.6,'
'How very Chekhovian of you, Herr Professor.'
'How foolish of you, Mr. Auden.'

Homage to Dylan Thomas.

Yet death did have some domain,
 Poets die young, and some older, Dylan,
your words went to heaven, I was in love with a boomed poetry
Not of stages or the world of fame,
We would not be mourned by dust,
For that random thud of our blood,
You are an immortal, poetic etching.

The turn to booze with a hazy gaze,
Morphine blued your gold mouth,
But dear Dylan, these poems are
 Not resplendent with a Welsh wit,
Yet trickle from tributaries of you,
With notions of your craft and art.

Dylan and Caitlin Thomas drink themselves into oblivion,
Let us dance with our dream of death. Grasp tightly together, tumble in tunnels, chanting to nil, cloaked zero, and chaos until freed from this frenzy of whirling fire.
We're stroked into sleep, a slumber of solitude.

Lines for Sappho.

Your heart is aflame with red desire,
Those offerings for a Helen of Troy,
Are wilted as you write of a lost lover,
Gone in your imaginations of flowers,
She had wandered Aphrodite's grove,
You had stroked my Aphrodite's buds.

A voice as sweet as flute at dewy dawn,
The music wrapping your beloved's body,
In her white linen robes so pure like desire,
 On Lesbos the Muses are singing with joy,
You write a verse of love, and lyres do play,
Yet a night still wails the song of loneliness.

I genuflected dumb before the poet's alter,
 And lay my back onto a willow netted cover,
For she is my eternal Eolian Harp, I write.

Narcissi and Red Roses.

Gusts of wind were howling around this white cube, a bare room.
I plucked veils of silver cobwebs from these shrouded, stinging and bloodshot eyes,
A globe of green satin was rolling around the floor in a mist of purple; at its burning Core was a priestess of Aphrodite, one of those who serve the cult of love on Lesbos, The isle where Sappho sings her spells. She began to celebrate Mass; I genuflected before her altar of withered narcissi, an aroma of sandalwood
was weaving like dust blown across a calm sea, this scent intoxicated our senses; my supplicant's hands were cupped in the form of a chalice before her,
she was peeling the petals from a red
Rose, they fluttered gently into a porcelain cup; it shattered into jagged pieces.

A Villanelle on the consequences of Sylvia Plath's first sighting of Ted Hughes.

Sylvia Plath could not stop cursing her writing
It was a mesh of death yet so divine,
Because she could never forget that first sighting.

One morning, Sylvia was faced with writing so biting.
She had to calm herself with some wine,

Sylvia Plath could not stop cursing her writing.

When she realised that the writing was exacting
She tried to focus on the pen line,
Because she could never forget that first sighting.

I tried to distract her with a strike of sun lightening
Said the mind she had was so fine,
Sylvia Plath could not stop cursing her writing.

Sylvia Plath decided to do something frightening.
The writing began to have a moonlit shine
Because she could never forget that first sighting.

As night drew on, her eyes were not enticing
Her mind had just begun to mime,
Sylvia Plath could not stop cursing her writing,
 Because she could never forget that first sighting.

For Sylvia Plath.

I am in your repose and so rest glad,
In that speckled rose budded grave,
A tomb, the canopy of willows wept,
Your purple soul just embraced me.

My pen is interwoven in caresses,
An entombed fragrance so sweet,
Ablaze with your lips red, purple,
My pen has murmured with Eros.

It scribes 'poetry is the blood jet.'

Padraig Anraí Mac Piarais. 1879-1916.

I rest without the dust of ages,
The grieves of my land lighter,
Now that the people listened,
And rebelled in the ballot box.

Anoint a bride and her groom,
Her land and his vaulted sky,
To walk to an alter so awaited,
My ring is placed on the land.

"The Fools, the fools, they have left us our Fenian dead, and while Ireland holds these graves, Ireland unfree shall never be at peace."
- Padraig Pearse.

Anna.

A blond goddess of the underground, of the revolution
 My back would be crisscrossed with ecstasy scratches,
Our first year crashed into that second, that Year Zero,
Posed as an urban guerrilla, you sold out the struggle.

A very nice lectureship with all the trimmings;
how do you Square the circle; perhaps you were always a little giddy
We were lost and bewildered, as no 'love in the struggle',
'Love is not enough; I need cash.' 'Goodbye', my reply.

The poem is composed while contemplating the coming harvest by the masses.

A harvest ready for our History's reaper, As we watch the death throes of Capital, It is dying while squirming and belching, The scythes grasped by the oppressed, Glistening steel catches the golden rays,
We have not forgotten the long dark nights of torment in homes, hospitals, and prisons.

The bourgeoisie are deformed, walking dead, Are mummified in the bondage of bandages?

Patients brandish the bayonets of Bolshevism, Hardened in the same foundries and factories As the unscabbarded swords of these masses, They are of the same furnace, a collective eye, The many in One omniscient gaze, we glared.

Us creatures are unbound, Herr Dr Frankenstein, Prometheans who carry the fiery plague to the rich, This is an antidote to all mind-numbing medicines, it is a revolution
To clear all that mind pollution of competitive evolution, The rats break free of your maze Dr Skinner, so exclaim: 'Oh no, they are misbehaving like those 'Homo sapiens.'

Unrhymed Sonnet.

They had an iron heart walking straight by a young girl in peril for her the street, There was no lion heart chivalric poem, A lady of withered flowers almost dead, They did not note the bum deal attempt, She pleaded 'tip me one mate', 'no way', Was his hissed reply, was she about 16? Her silent scream, that sea of salt sobs.

This dumb poet had his heart ripped out,
I knew that girl thirty-odd clean years ago, Illusions we never had as 'smack' we did; dreamscapes have that shimmering logic, Entombed in a body with no umbilical cord,
The dealer's grey grimace had severed it.

In the Laboratory.

Red tentacles are gripping the wasted wail of a seething brain which writhes in
delirium with a rush, white light
C H N10 15
Eyes hang loose, attached only by yellow threads to grey sockets; they melted a millisecond ago and now are dripping,
Dropping by diamond drop into a culture dish, the doctor makes a smear, Places a slide beneath the lens of a microscope and peers in,
A banshee screams into her eyes; she jumps back too late,
The laboratory rotates into concentric circles; it has become a phantasmagoria; that pain had gone; the chemical lights blazed, but she had lost her mind, insane.

 Note: C H N10 15 is the formula for methamphetamine (Methedrine).

A meditation on Andy Warhol's 'Factory'.

Many had entered this company of the joyful and mad because they wrote when amphetamine had hammered. They were sucked into a dark room, dragged in, then spewed out when in pain; some fixed and rapidly wrote,
Others painted after a hit; some wailed their ink or paint onto paper like orgasms of
A moon's second rising: others were green-eyed with their claws extended, Scratching each other in the desert and simultaneously drunk from an oasis; their straight and profane families of mistrust were crucified and sacrificed, Coffined so permitting poets and artists to descend from their cross without showing their bruised stigmata.

Some wandered and wised their way out, went to labyrinths of communes as hashish somnambulists, but alert; they kept a pen and paper within reach. A Barbiturate bard had been taught to fumble, stumble, and mumble; he claims: 'I can recall and write about their verse and the hearse of that Methedrine Ark'.

'This is Doctor Death calling', my friend had said.
(a prose poem).

The room had not been cleaned since this speed binge began around nine months ago. It was a mess; empty cartons of orange juice speckled the floor as we had tried to maintain our health with Vitamin C. All of us were mainlining in excess of two grams of high-quality amphetamine sulfate daily and nightly because we did not sleep. As you may or may not be able to imagine, the line between everyday consciousness and the surreal becomes more and more blurred until it disappears. Throw into that cauldron an array of psychedelics, and the unconscious was the realm in which we resided. Any poetry, which was written, and art created, was like an Ego in this ocean of Id. This state of mind was a desired consequence. Unfortunately, the scene was not only composed of writers and artists, but as time went on, even some of the creatives were beginning to degenerate into hedonism, but it was changing and deteriorating. One day or night, who knew, as they merged into one another, I saw a man, almost a skeleton with giant protruding eyeballs, his thyroid had gone, jack up a straight gram of sulfate, flush, fill the syringe with blood, whack the blood up as well. Still, he pulled back the white plastic plunger and filled the 'works' with blood again, leapt to his feet, and spurted the blood onto the white emulsion ceiling. It was really crazy, man. Another young man had been

trembling in the corner with a blanket over his
head and shoulders, making occasional whining
sounds: 'give me speed, man, I need speed, man.'
My friend with whom I had discussed everything
from the Dhammapada to Nietzsche yelped: 'man,
this is really far-in, you know what I mean.' I
replied, 'far-out, man, just far-out.'

Then he was consumed by something; I had never
known what possessed him,
maybe his brain had finally dissolved. He loaded
several syringes with speed and
moved like a spectre around the shimmering
room. He injected one after another and said each
time: 'This is Doctor Death calling….'

On hearing of the death of a hippy.
Turn on, tune in, and drop out.
-Timothy Leary.

That herd were thronging back and forth;
While I rolled along the old academic slot,
Not unaware of a lime green undercurrent,
The radar is still finely tuned, so inevitably

Street woman flies along on crystal crutches.
She stops dead 'Arthur is dead morphine O.D.',
Those buttresses of ice melt, and we embrace,
'I am going to see him in the chapel I am now.'

She is skimming heaven on crystal meth;

how Long has she got, I shake, for they are blessed;
he was a gentle shadow-man who always said,
The same lines about some Nirvana or I-Ching.

Each death is scratched on my heart; it bleeds.

A man became an egg; (a surrealist poem).

There was a spectral man who hid in a physical frame; He roamed like a grounded vulture across the concrete. There was no harvest of gold corn or pleasant deer too
Inspire the poet here, only the arched acridness of the herd, Junkies huddled in alleyways wailing with their junk sickness, The thin and translucent membrane formed herself around And the man touched a tingling rebirth; she had encrusted

Herself but eggshells are thin,
Egg boxes never are quite right like paper-mâché disintegrating in the rain; The shell shattered, so she dissolved herself and became the yellow yoke.

Already an artist with eyes like black oceans had painted the egg in beautiful
gold and blue,
He ate this egg; a yolk flowed out dark as bitter blood into the pen of the poet. That poet then wrote like a serpent who has just been uncoiled, tongue licking.

A beam of hope that year: on the curing of a terminal physical illness.

A death pyre fire was a flame that burned throughout two thousand, and fourteen,

The stench of my burning flesh accompanied each breath, and essay any poem scribed,
I was intoxicated and revolted by the odours of my post-addiction, this a dance of death, Thirty years clean and dry, degrees,
poetry and prose published have all been so cruel.

A new treatment and the consultant had agreed. It was like the rising sun aglow, fondling my brain
And stroking what was the darkest of our nights
Because this was not the Dark Night of the Soul,
No, it would have been the oblivion of the tomb,
For there is not any belief in resurrection here.

Together with the medics and new antivirals, New dawn, the albatross flies from my ship.

The Bluebottle.

A blue bottle was buzzing so bloody loudly; Boris, darling Boris, you have saved us all. It dipped too low than desired for workers, Go away, hey ho, buzz off away or… We spray the true-blue fly with insecticide, no lift red swot and thwack twat take that, the dustbin of History opens to the rest of that swarm.
Crawl flies, beetles, lemmings to your doom,   For ours is the dawn, the morning and noon.

To an unnamed person.

In a country graveyard, there are many quenched words,
The words of love and hatred and forgotten pleasures,
The laments of the hollow Dead and their demented wails,
And yes, words of love which remained spoken, silenced.

A family torn asunder by malicious powers, forces so darkly,
You had wallowed in the unhallowed ceremonies of midnight,
But play with fire, and you get burnt, but so do the innocents,
 A saccharine smile fooled so many, yourself but not a priest.

We say this incantation to exorcise those fiery Dante demons:
> "Vade retro Satana."

As you had said: 'I can fool any doctor, but I cannot fool you.'

They should have enforced the leukotomy for everyone's sake,
 For your demons could not simply be cast into a herd of swine.

The tale of a mother and her son (a narrative poem).

The Prologue.

In our beginning was pitch, infinite darkness,
There Isis conceived this sun-dazzled Icarus, Isis,
my mother, a fountain of Spring, Winter's Frozen
wasteland, you wept me into a genesis, It was
here we feasted on fruit that fell from the
Sacred Tree, then staggering drunk
With love and hate, we embraced clouds of gold.
We settled on the border of this chiming Garden;
This dance was enacted before the silver Serpent,
Wanderers of the Psyche, mother, was a Jewess
of the soul rather than the blood.
Grasped my hand and guided me from the
Garden, There the Serpent's tongue had licked
shut our eyes, We roamed hazy peaks and
caverns of biting dreams, Until this child was cast
in a mould, set, yet still molten With lava that
spewed from the Fall's ancient volcano, This river
burned furrows in our minds, two souls which
Had journeyed alone were one in the fire, like
intoxication, We wandered with Psyche, who is
unfathomable love.

Icarus soared.

The awakening screwed into this sun-dazzled Icarus; I wept as mother entered the labyrinth of dazed lies, So leapt out of that snare, the trap of enclosed terror,

Focused on the poetry of psychedelia and joyfulness, Visions I saw in the sky and soul whispered into the sun, I soared and caressed the gaze of a Serpent of silver,
In suspended heaven, these waxen eyes had melted, Dripped, and dropped by a crystal into a sea of frosted glass. To freeze the milieu of those "straights", they follow zero.

Mother dies.

The black clams of Time stuck onto mum's frail body; those rusty chains of age and illusion bound her mind. She spiraled inwards in an introspective frenzy of sparks. As her autumn leaves were blown into the chill of Winter,
I walked with her and her ghosts in that becalmed odyssey. Slimy Sea monsters would rise and frighten us; both children, Mum and I, would sit in the House of Dementia; she sat hunched
And meditating on the coloured interwoven threads of her memories, The wind blew her, that crumpled paper Buddha, away into infinity.

The icebox: a prose-poem.

This is a box within a box, a world within a world, and a house typical of many in suburbia. It is brown-bricked, anonymous, and almost transmits hymns of praise to some tarnished copper god of mediocrity. In the kitchen of this house stands a fridge; it looks white and prosaic. Open the fridge door, and at the top on the right is a sky-blue icebox; it has three white stars to confirm the adequacy of its freezing capacity. Inside the icebox is a rectangular tray divided into squares; each can be filled with water and frozen to produce the perfect ice cube. This can then be dropped into a frosted pink glass that wraps around it, fruit juice, and the ideal chilled drink. A son frequently opens the fridge door, pulls down the sky-blue icebox flap, and peeps inside. He examines the frosted walls, which, paradoxically, burn his fingers; they are almost burnt with the coldness. In this world of ice cubes, he discovers another dimension that exists separately from but is intrinsically attached to the ebb and flow of everyday life. The son's mother had died some years ago. The son had an unusual relationship with the ice cubes in the fridge, finding great comfort in popping two out from the tray and holding them in his hands until they were numb and the ice cubes dissolved into water. The living room of this box within the box was bare, with no carpet, furnishings, or pictures. However, glaring at him was a gas fire. It had short brown steel legs at each end to support it. A copper pipe stuck up through the floorboards and was connected to the fire. The fire was coloured in two tones of brown, light brown at the bottom and around the sides of the gas jets and dark brown above. The shelf, which was on top of the whole apparatus and rested against the wall, had white plastic knobs at each end; one was to turn on and ignite.

The other was to control the gas flow to regulate the temperature. This fire concerned the son greatly; it almost dominated him. He didn't like the hissing of the gas or the flickering flames, and the brief smell of gas at ignition caused him much anxiety. He felt little or no choice but to constantly check and check again that the gas was burning correctly and there was no leak. With the certainty of the tides, his life became enslaved to this gas fire. The only respite was allowing the ice cubes to melt in his hands. Just as the season's motion is inevitable, the gas fire developed a leak. Fortunately, the son was elsewhere when the explosion tore through the house, destroying it and its anonymity. It no longer looked like all the other houses in the cul-de-sac. The fridge was severely damaged and thought to no longer fulfil any practical task; it was taken to the local tip. The ice cubes turned into water, but a more profound metamorphosis occurred: a voice said: 'My son, there is no longer any need to worry.' The water had leaked from the icebox and out of the fridge into the rubbish of the tip in which it germinated as a seed planted at the beginning of Time. In Spring, the shoot may push its way up and bloom into pure snowdrops.

Will, the jackbooted ones, march through the tip
and crush in blind But ordered fury this flower and
any hope of its delicate flourishing.

I am breaking down and breaking through.

When we can see beyond the tokens of things, To
penetrate those masks of men and women, And
lift those veils that most are hidden behind, A child
with an all-devouring mouth and eyes.

This collapse could renounce a communicant's
Belief in the Host and hurl into Dantesque hell;
Here, we will meet forgotten selves and ghosts,
Twisted in agonies of reabsorption into the ego.

But a doctor, not today a priest, may intervene,
That keeper of the profane apothecary exorcise,
Unlike Hildegard, Julian, those medieval mystics,
We are not celebrated but are instead shackled.

For today there is not the adoration of madmen;
instead, the projection of your fears onto them.

Autumnal.

This season of mellow fruitfulness, the apples were teeming with termites,
That Tree who held a fruit of temptation called knowledge is now rotten,
Earth, whose roots clasp and grasp, is frozen like a leaden bronze sky.

Adam lies in the depths of a cider vat; he had waved, drunk and drowned,
The leeches replace manacles on his mind, and his body is now wormed,

A howler of hurricanes tossed the loose leaves; laughter was lost too soon,
The woman who kicked her way through the shades of brown and crimson,
She fled in a flurry of rustling colour, and Eve escaped the Garden gladly.

No verse is free for the man who wants to do a good job.'
   - T. S. Eliot (1957) On Poetry and Poets, p.37.

Lines on writing poetry through the prism of schizo-affective disorder.

My poetry can fling into flights of flurries, any figurative phantom,
Demon, Ghoul, Ghost or Spectre,
I wrenched these words from a brain seething with purple worms,

Those 'mind-forged manacles' melt like icicles without my volition.

It is into that prism
 this wild poetry must be...
Refracted through an undulating optic of a preordained iconoclast,
To make this unmade poetry into something so precise, ordered,
I must ease my mind into a straitjacket, a mould of concrete, clay.

Now, these devils, ghouls, ghosts, and spectres become coaxed
Into The Common Reader, but I am not in Virginia Woolf's class,
She was born above me in both wealth, status and was a genius.

Note. Woolf, Virginia (2003) [ed] Andrew MacNeille, The Common Reader Vols 1 & 2 London, Vintage. These were a collection of literary essays initially published in 1925 and 1932, respectively.

Studies in syllabics.

Winter Haiku.

Ice has formed across
A lone pool, words are crying
Beneath its smooth face.

Haiku in madness.

Madness exhales breath
To lift veils, there the sane gasp
For they have no air.

Two classes, two poetics, a Marxist Ars Poetica.

'Understanding the poem is not only an intellectual act but a political act.'
- Frantz Fanon, The Wretched of the Earth.
They seem like an eagle, then swoop
Like a vulture in search of its carrion,
The width of that cloth matters to you
As you blather with pounds sterling.

You pose with a jewel-encrusted pen
Which is dry, no ink oozed from its nib,
We forged a nib of the masses in steel
With lightning strikes and thunderclaps.

Writes on papyrus, parchment, and paper,
The internet also hums as part of this kit,
We have many pens, but who holds them?
Scribes, sleepers, scholars, and workers.

One History but two classes, two poetics,
They clash with sparks; they are cymbals
In History's echo chamber, softly or noisily,
Then the Albert Hall crumbles as we sing

Until we are no longer like Robinsonades,
But resonate with a verse woven by us all,
So, multiplicities of pens write on the page,
This is the linen soaked in blood, our flag.

For whom the bell tolls. (A political poem).

> Perchance, he for whom this bell tolls may be so ill, as that he knows not it tolls for him.
> - John Donne.

Etonian bankers bark orders wrapped in gold leaf,
In vestments of Capital, the suits with twisted ties,
Lays with defrocked priests, a smirking Pharisee,
But sighs with a pleated moan in Downing Street.

Britannia tacks in choppy seas with winds groaning,
Beware because you are not a mirage, anachronism,
The lava of the oppressed is bubbling up in oceans,
It will sweep the dust out of that empty opera house.

Bourgeois end that obscene ballet with cut-out dolls,
You are now dancing with terrible tolls of death bells,
Begins to ring in their ears, weep, wince, and whine,
As the proletariat strikes, a black panther on its prey.

Panther's patrol streets the vanguard of red stars,
People live freely now as dollars have burnt, died,
The oppressors are tin soldiers who had rusted,
The Festival of the Oppressed is like a rainbow.

Let those living dead return to their catacombs,
While we fill these wineskins with clean waters.

A detained teenage political prisoner in a psychiatric hospital in the 1970s.

A poem of witness.
A monk on another ward also conversed on
Tim Leary and Che, so we colluded,
Nurses without eyes, just film covered ones

Presumed purveyors of darker arts,
This poet wrote in metaphors not grasped by
those who had crawling sedated minds,
Doctors had theories as children are born
in bell-jars of discontent, no need to worry.

Then clientele spat sputum into cardboard

Spittoons not emptied, but flung in rage,
Doctors hid them in wards with sycophants

Faces like brick-and-mortar monotone,
A nurse wanted patients to be aborted cherubs of
heaven. But were like banshees,
No one dared mention the death of a young victim,
as things were hot in those hells.

'Take over the asylum and make it a red campus':
howled the interned revolutionary,
Just play bingo, pleaded Janus nurse as he
winked at some wincing nurse students,
The patients leapt like tigers, so that panzer squad
prepared a spikey chemical cosh,
All had electro-convulsive therapy called Terror
afterwards as the wires just buzzed.

Not forgotten were those whose deaths in
Stammheim Prison had left a bitter taste,
Ulrike, Gudrun, and Andrea's suicide in the
securest prison ever built, possibly not,
Bitter is a taste of lemon; lemon is yellow that will
colour if cancer strikes in the liver,
Red is our funeral shroud because cowardice
does not glaze those jaundiced eyes.
Note 1. "red campus" during the early 1970s, the
orthodox British Trotskyist organisation,
International Marxist Group, adhered to a position
that if they gained control of the universities. It
would then be possible to spread the revolution to
the proletariat.

Note 2.
Ulrike Meinhof, Gudrun Ensslin & Andreas Baader
were founding members of the West German
Leftist urban guerrilla group, Red Army Faction.
They died in suspicious circumstances within
Stammheim high-security prison, which housed
RAF prisoners.

A poem in Blank Verse upon reading Tara Bergin:

The Tragic Death of Eleanor Marx (Revised).
'Understanding the poem is not only an intellectual act but a political act.'
   - Frantz Fanon, The Wretched of the Earth

A cloth with width is what matters
Because you seethe with dollars,
As you are lost, then seek trophies
As vultures search for their carrion.

A jewel-encrusted pen you posture
With is dry, no ink oozed from its nib,
The nib of masses is forged in steel
In bloody sounds with a thunderclap.

It writes on papyrus, parchment, paper,
The internet is also a willow in the wind,
We have many pens, but who holds them,
Scribes, sleepers, scholars, and workers.

One History but two classes, two poetics,
They clash with sparks, as are cymbals
In History's echo chamber, soft or noisily
Until the chamber crumbles, a new song.

Then we will not be like Robinsonades,
But resonate with a verse made by all.
 Dmitritch Gromov on Ward No.6 in the asylum. (a prose/concrete poem).

My name is Ivan, and I address you from a ward in the asylum. I was merely sat huddled in an overcoat observing a streetlamp; it was hanging with my mind from the moon.

This room is like a block of ice,
 A pixilated light is scolding my eyes
 I pick up my blanket and try to block out the moonshine,
Because the moon is scornful of my mind,
I remove this rag of a blanket; the lunar light glimmers again and bounces off these walls; it drowns me. Morning

 Mutters outside the room. A big polished black boot kicks open the door and crush me as if I were a piece of origami. There is also pelting sleet outside
That burns me like the pain from the blow of that boot,
It burns like the Sulphur in Dante's Inferno.

It is finger-numbingly cold in their inferno.
They may believe I have a torn and twisted heart.
No, it is not cold but convoluted and complex like a puzzle. I run from this room, feel the water, and feel the rain, icy as if spurting from a frozen geyser in Siberia. Fall to the ground, the Earth, with a splat. I am instantaneously frozen. I was never in any doubt that their heart was true blue, cold like the sky hanging across Antarctica.
My body had been forcibly frozen.
Once placed in a crossbow, a steel arrow can pierce the hottest soul in a stiff straitjacket. When

this bolt haemorrhages those blue people, they
will be as if nothing pure zero.
That foul smell of decay in a wilderness,
Which will be blown away by a wild wind,
Dr Andrey Ragin, join us in this struggle,
Now, you have no choice in the asylum.

You see the peril of reading Chekhov.
Two poets contemplate Salvador Dali:
The Persistence of Memory. (An ekphrasis).
https://www.moma.org/collection/works/79018

Their mind is opening like a
lotus flower stung

By a spear of reed,
her breath drifts in lemon

Globules, pupils are fixed on
a door which is woven

From willow branches, he opens an
aperture to discover

A zone that interacts
with her black eyes, leaden

In the midst of lunar storms, they
embrace, bodies are like

Cotton pages blown across a sea covered in silver
scales, until wrapped

In a ball of silk, they exhale rhythmically
with the pulse of the Earth, the clock faces have
melted.

A Shakespearian Sonnet to a modern Mary Magdeleine.

Their breath was silk and choked with sin,
Her gloss black boots of leather mock him,
A fascist complete with a whip to discipline,
He curls into a ball before the bloody hymn.
That strap was raised just like a Nazi play,
It cracks with whacks like goose-step troops,
They do not love like sheep who come Sunday,
But you and I know the song of our troupes.
Our Lady of Sorrows forgot to shut the bars,
Had drunk with those sad, mad, and bad men,
But fell on streets to gaze at dim-lit mist stars,
Tried Mass but heard Nietzsche's madman.
If God is dead, mirage, you have a vocation,
Maybe shadows of fire whisper edification.

The Tenth Muse in a man's world:
responses to Patriarchy in poetry.

A Sonnet (Shakespearean) for Anne Sexton.

Those hands began to write a page with dew,
Her heart had shed the haunts and bonds of Light,
She turned and smiled to cast a spell, this guru,
So tense until her pen began to write…
A verse of storms, angels of night who share,
Her seas of lavender wept waves of wonder,
The sun had raised so redly to kiss her hair,
She sat quite still and breathed like Buddha.
Her wine could sweeten bitter potions,
But doctors, the priests of modernity
 Are glaring flames; her poems were emotions,
They scorched them with shocks of electricity,
These burnt into her heart of love, your mind,
 A soul was numbed by barbiturate and lay blind.

For Elise Cowen (1933-1962), a Shakespearean Sonnet.

Your smile it shone with clouds we call our verse,
You glimpse the straights in cars with an iris blur,
And gaze at Forms they drive in their cracked hearse,
For you who dance stark words without murmur.
The peace of wombs was like a coiled temptress,
Our wastes we walk without that veiled humour,
A moth flew into the night which was sadness,
A flame that burnt your wings had no candour.
I cupped and scattered you in morning dew,
You wrote the lamentations of the desert,
A mind was sane in that cruellest mildew,
The strength in the syringe was just like dirt.
It is here that some lie stillborn in the womb,
I dig in graves in search of your lost tomb.

I was Simone de Beauvoir's lost child.
I was made for another planet altogether. I mistook the way.
> — Simone de Beauvoir, The Woman Destroyed, 1969.

My mother and I ached with the beauty of Beethoven, which caressed our minds,
Where else could an Appassionata Sonata be played but bliss in those heavens,
Aphrodite chained to a cruel cross, yes, our love was crucified, and it bleeds red,
Neither of us was of the world, which we assumed belonged to ghost nightmares,
We celebrated our love of poetry and philosophy, you Muse of past, the present,
My wings, contorted wax had whipped up a tempest that you thought so terrible,
That you and your butterfly heartbeat for me fluttered away one summer's night,
It went straight back to the planet forsaken and drowned in a sea of gold coins,
An ornate veil hid a petrified perfection that brute with the boot and book bought.

Now my mind screamed, and blood runs sour as there is no beebread to nourish,
I am an amphibian without wings, gliding, sliding through endless waves of pages,
Solitary creature shunned by a world, a hermit in a wasteland of theses and writing,
This slime is like primaeval sludge
for Leary gave the trips,
Sartre the amphetamine,

Leary would mangle the world, Sartre 'lit up his mind', your ideas were like lightning.

Summer of love, 1967. (a neo-villanelle).

Time melts thawed a frosty reality to dissolve ice without a stumble,
Our eyes, whose dilated pupils could swallow any hardened gaze,
(You fell across this hallucinogenic Cosmos, those stars humble).

We crucified the betrayal of damned love and stared so terrible,
That dark spark we conceived was like evaporating into a haze,
Time melts thawed a frosty reality to dissolve ice without a stumble,

I touched with delicate fingers the clasp on your eyes to unbuckle,
A stream, the purple fragrance of humming, a goddess was ablaze,
(You fell across this hallucinogenic Cosmos, those stars humble).

You crumpled in a sphere of sighs encircled by Light only to sparkle,
Whose wings were caressed, and we dived into the sun in a daze,
Time melts thawed a frosty reality to dissolve ice without a stumble.

Our song was vibrating into weeping trees, nectar dripping, suckle,
The other's ancient milk, which is a sacred libation with our praise,

(You fell across this hallucinogenic Cosmos, these stars humble).

Tangerine gasp intertwines in a frenzy of breath and falls in a trickle,
Then we lie exhausted in a grave, bodies consumed yet they raise,
Time melts thawed a frosty reality to dissolve ice without a stumble,
(You fell across this hallucinogenic Cosmos, those stars humble).

An incarnation of Sappho and her friend accidentally OD.

Some yell with spite and call it love, but not us, not in a temple of Aphrodite. Here Sappho tends a flame which brushes her lips; they are burning and red … now purple as the heroin hit hard like a hammer thumping its heat up the arm into the galaxy of welcoming brain cells. The hypodermic hangs limply from her arm, I gently draw the spike out of the bruised vein, her arm flops diagonally across an orange cotton shirt, I clean the syringe by rhythmically flushing water in and out and then Finally, squirt the crimson juice into a blue china
 Bowl: next, prepare my hit; we uncurl in a temple Of Aphrodite, which is where lovers can purr softly,
the floor opens like a gaping mouth and gobbles
                both of us
                    UP.

The ghost of Ulrike Meinhof addresses the bourgeoisie.
(Ulrike Meinhof 1934-1976.)

Our waves will wash away the sand into a sea,
Bourgeois fuckers, your system is screwed,
Ripped off the poor and the tenants,
   A hot and dry summer will scorch with fire and now burn baby burn.

Think you are stable, no just sinking into an ocean of Narcissism which is not pretty,
never learn bourgeois,
Now your houses are being repossessed, and those mind's twang:
      those robbed of their dreams now awake;
you will be shaking in your shoes as the ghettos buzz,
  Start to tremble you have failed, and now the red revolutionary Nemesis awaits.
The Angry Brigade is aware and alert, and the Red Army Faction has not forgotten,
Socialist Patients Collective flex their minds, and their trigger-fingers are twitching,
Do not think that the Red Brigades are all banged up inside.

Our waves will wash away the sand into a sea,
Bourgeois fuckers, your system is screwed,
Ripped off the poor and the tenants,
  A hot and dry summer will scorch with fire and now burn baby burn.

They were so astonished, astounded that a member of the intelligentsia became an Urban guerrilla.
Ulrike, they exhumed your brain after a dreaded death to try and solve their puzzle.

Greek partisans. [A villanelle].

The dawn awakes, we are cloaked in snow,
Snow melts to leave bare and bleak terrain,
 My cloak is red, unlike that of a black crow.

This morning I know that knife will glow,
 I shall shake with shame, with the stain,
The dawn awakes, we are cloaked in snow,

Some do not know the heaving lava below,
Or seasonal cruelty with that brutal blame,
My cloak is red, unlike that of a black crow.

A vocation of pain the shepherds do know,
We herd the innocents and see their pain,
The dawn awakes, we are cloaked in snow,

No, do not bow to that ancient status quo,
An act of revolt she who could never fain,
My cloak is red, unlike that of a black crow.

In Greek hills, our blood must always flow,
For Sappho, the struggle has a bloodstain,
The dawn awakes, we are cloaked in snow,
My cloak is red, unlike that of a black crow.

Lost for words with Wordsworth. Constructed from 'found' passages in William Wordsworth: Preface to Lyrical Ballads & The Prelude.

Poetry is the spontaneous outpouring
of emotion, bliss it was to be alive yet
to be young was very heaven, when
recollected in tranquillity as a prelude.

The Sonnet was written by a latter-day Katherine Philips (1632-1664).
    (author of Against Love).

Should I compare you to a statue of steel,
My sheep know this is a time of delusion,
At Mass, they fear to feast upon the meal,
We dry our sea of tears without an illusion.
That hum of minds was like a bloody buzz,
He was a wire on fire like a ghost on gas,
Our school of thought was not jiving jazz,
The man with radar that zooms into cash.
His type is not for us because we fought,
Remained in banks like a painted clown,
He became green, the dollar was bought,
The tide has turned; we gazed and frown.
The God who reads these wise finite lines,
I have a fear of Him for I know those signs.

Psychiatric nurses try reading some Dostoevsky.

The psychiatric nurse always wears a smile of roses,
 But when she opens her mouth, only the thorns show,
They rip into us like mercury is rising up a thermometer,
But we are Mercury; we are those messengers of words,
Communication is sanity until an abyss stare's back at us,
Our emotional temperature is wrong, perceptions askew,
So chant the nurses as they prostrate themselves before

'THE SELF'

In its glory and feel one of the few, a mental health professional,
We break the shackles on the nurse's ego and drag them from
Their shallows of grey bourgeois murk, then, quite the reaction,
They have a deranged duck moment of insight here and incisive
Understanding there a magic diagnosis, nurse read Dostoevsky,
Just step into a world of underground people as you amuse us.

To an anonymous woman poet met in 1941.

This woman is manna on the breeze,
And is the wind that plays my chimes,
The hands that play and stroke a harp,
You hold both an ancient quill and pen.

She welcomes with warmth, shy, sharp,
Responds with moonbeams on her lips,
But memory is like some tightened strap,
The heat of summer melts those buckles.

Fingernails dig into her temple of a body,
Mine just resembles your twisted shrine,
The tubes of lace are torn and ruptured,
It began to seep out, the yellowish fog.

We can only taste that creeping aroma,
The cyanide pellets crushed intoxicate,
She, my lunar soliloquist, has departed,
I choke on vapour, a last gasp grasped.

Our Lady of Sorrows in Notting Hill Gate (1973)

That green-scaled goddess of grief how she is wailing from her brown soil grave,
It is here that the recently resurrected dead exchange their laughter without any lament,
But you, who are skeletal with yellow skin pulled tight in a smile of delight, you,
A beatified Courtesan who roams these connected on electrified tuned-in grids,
A heart wrapped in sackcloth, which is worn by those incipient lovers of chaos,
Here a frozen embryo begins to pulsate, it breaths with the bitter pulp of those
apples bit in the Garden of Pleasure,
Ice folds into our eyes until lost we are reborn into this spectrum of zoned silence,
I embrace you; you took the crucifixion from my eyes, and our eyes do bleed bliss.

Morpheus and William Burroughs (a Petrarchan sonnet.)

We groove along furrows to cut the wet pavement,
This street reflects an inner web, this glassy maze,
The path to oblivion, it melts like an echo of praise,
The temple begins to sing with an awaking ferment,
The dream-powder, its magic is like night's scent,
A garden of delight where sight and tears are glazed.
You spike the mainline again; this is not so crazed,
 The cobweb is caught like a dream's finite content.

But Morpheus is a cruel god, in darkness confess,
His bonds, we know his mellow, like a nocturne,
 We were naked, our mind's flow does dissolve,
 A cloud whose rain which beats us nails, Venus
Always burns away my colours in eyes not taciturn,
 What remains, the riddles of thought, always turn?

A beat moment in a Beat life: A dramatic monologue.

Those square hearts had stopped,
they were
Just rusty bilge pumps,
someone had turned
Their switch off, what a turn-on
We never dug that scene with America,
The atom bombs, we chant with those
Of us who had a different sound
and song to the hooded-snake death dirge,
breathe the snow
wind of pure purgation, howl cathartic baby
burnout buzz madness.

William placed enigma in caps, opened that cap,
cooked it, fixed it, again, hazy.

DECONDITIONED OURSELVES FROM STATE SUBLIMINAL MANIPULATION,
Bill had a sweet-death golden flight of Icarus, that perpetual labour of Sisyphus,
I missed your tube shit there goes a decent rush, blood looks very dark, hepatitis?

Unlike us, Allen, some did get clean, but their purple lights remain floating free.

Speaking of viral poetry: a prose poem.

> Language is a virus from outer space...The author is simply a node on a network, through which ideas pass.
> - William Burroughs, The Ticket that Exploded, 1962.

That fatigue can no longer frighten us like the ice sheets in mind, it is beyond any vestige or manifestation of fear as glaring of sun drills eyes. The black petals begin to fold inwards when a gaze is or isn't fixed, tangles of twisted thorns of a tight thistle bush are forests of emptiness, viral poetry is written and formed into lakes of ice, from ice is refined the pure crystals that are polished into those old cold stars, they had imploded long ago creating the gulping black holes. Babies' mouths who drink from a nipple which oozes dark milk, it's ancient not nectar, it is the ingestion of the 'Other', us as a dark subject, objectification is unmade. Promenaded people wake up and do not think black holes are empty, scabby fingers are grasping the bourgeois hand that shivers with revulsion, grey-suited exorcists wail 'demon get out', but we existed for aeons before Eden or logos; our word is an infectious virus. For you are totally helpless, we have convinced your best philosophers since Epicurus and inspired the poet Sappho, then lit the fuse around October 1917. We are the Virus made word, made material in your universe because our cells have penetrated it.

A poem for William Burroughs.

I saw the best minds of my generation destroyed by madness, starving hysterical naked, dragging themselves through the streets at dawn looking for a fix.

 - Allen Ginsberg, Howl, 1956.

 Staring streets reflect the voids in your eyes which are mirrors of the squares,
They exist without the pricking needle easing chaos; you found the mainline again,
An embrace like an orgasm burning through a vein, Zen with and without the hassle,
This Light strikes those chemical cells calling calmly to the soul like that whispered
welcome of nothingness,
The Absurdity is not in these oceans where weeping tranquillity tumbles into dreams for you were dancing into the masquerades of non-being.
High womb-like peace sleep, wake, write, weep, fix again. You survived, died at 83 because being you, you always 'went first'.

Summer of love, 1967. (a villanelle).

Time melts: we thawed a frosty reality to dissolve ice with our love,
Our eyes whose dilated pupils could swallow any hardened gaze,
(You fell across this hallucinogenic Cosmos, these stars tumble).

We crucified the betrayal of damned love and stared to humble.
 That dark spark, we conceived this just like evaporating into a haze,
 Time melts: we thawed a frosty reality to dissolve ice with our love,

 I touched with delicate fingers the clasp on your eyes to unbuckle.
A stream, the purple fragrance of humming, a goddess was ablaze,
 (You fell across this hallucinogenic Cosmos, these stars tumble).

You crumpled into a sphere of sighs encircled by white Light, a dove,
 Whose wings were caressed as we dived into the sun in a daze,
Time melts: we thawed a frosty reality to dissolve ice with our love.

Our song was vibrating into weeping trees, nectar dripping, suckle,
 The other's ancient milk, which is a sacred libation with soft praise,

(You fell across this hallucinogenic Cosmos, these stars tumble).

Tangerine gasp intertwines in a frenzy of breath, it falls from above,
Then we lie exhausted in a grave, our bodies consumed, but raised,
Time melts: we thawed a frosty reality to dissolve ice with our love.

Prose-poem to 'tribunes of the oppressed' when 'clean'.

Man was born free, and he is everywhere in chains. Those who think themselves the masters of others are indeed greater slaves than they.
— Jean-Jacques Rousseau, The Social Contract, 1762.

The moon rises like mist distilled from a burnt river to whirl with her humming until the bonds unravel. Now she is caressing her smile into the radiant morning; her dust is lingering it sprinkles onto dormant souls of night awaking our song of love to a golden dawn. The poet's pen is dipping into this chalice of Light we wander across pages with infinity and innocence. Dance with the Light and shadows of the sacred ritual, this is a Psalm of joy to a pristine moon and drowsy sun, you and I, humanity.

Yet she and he know the multitudes remain in shackles, some of iron, steel, or gold. Not until we 'tribunes of the oppressed' have severed, sawn every fetter can we rest.

Haiku.
A pillar of stone
Has a cloak of golden light.
It wraps itself in.

Haiku on poets.
Cut our mind of coils
 And it bleeds an ink of joy.
That stain lemon stars.

Again, for Sylvia Plath.

I am in your repose rested in a speckled rose grave,
>A tomb in a canopy of willows weeping,
Your bejewelled soul is purple and enticing my fountain
>>pen weaves willow within it.

An entombed fragrance can be so sweetly stoned,
>Ablaze with your lights legal and purple,
My pen murmured and ejaculated on a page
>>'poetry is the blood jet.'
>>You said.

An Elegy for Graham upon pondering W. H. Auden
Musee des Beaux-Arts, 1938.

Ablaze this Icarus fell from the ticked time,
Auden missed the point in that 1938 rhyme,
I heard your voice aloud in the baying pack
Of mental nurses, they walk with a whack.

A cut of words was sharp and yelled aloud,
You spoke with Laing and chanted so proud,
We told of a world of flowers and revolution,
The staff still smear us; they have no solution.

Phone erupted, and anonymity croaked death,
A slip of the tongue, just Freudian foul breath,
Could be a trap set by those greened eyed,
My abbey echoed with words sighs it cried.

And death has dominion; it drinks with a thirst,
That silver chalice has wine which is our dust.

Another Adonis.

Looked into your eyes and saw a galaxy of stars,
They glared like an untameable beam of death,
Like your beloved Lennard Cohen words were
Almost like syllables roughed, coughed, howled,
A cheetah glanced out of the shadow but always
Would purr in imperfect pulses in that asymmetry,
But whoever wanted to be a square like a sheep?

There was a disequilibrium in your pure metre,
Always the day dawned and danced its words,
We waltzed our minds into a cloud of unknowing.

The scroll did not roll out for the staid sane pens,
Our pens etched souls of amber wrote the words
That reverberated like loss and love petrification,
 We made pyres of words, tried to purge the pain.

A Tiger.

A tiger burnt cold as he circled a herd of zebra,
I await his next stitch as there is always a needle,
It starts with moves and little drinky poos for free,
But nothing is free with him, too long behind bars

Of pubs and prisons, a peppermint crème oozes,
Now he has charmed again 'have these Blues,'
His insurance policy whirled into one more oasis,
Why does he decide to deceive the stripy flocks?

Because he has nothing to fool within but a void,
Avoid I would if it were at all possible as it bores,
What of 'tribunes of the oppressed' if not when?
But herds of zebra are dispensable as not lions.

I guess a 'crash-pad' is better than the streets,
Shame about the zebra though.

But do you not blink at their gangrene gouged
Limbs,
Those ordered lines of stigmata upon stigmata,

    It all started with little drinky poos.

He remembered Elise Cowen and glanced three times at a lightbulb.
(A prose-poem.)

He sits in a sea of yellow custard cushions observing a solitary lightbulb. It is suspended, dangles like his mind, by a single withered cord. It is pulsating slightly, or so it seems; no, it is the bulb flickering. The room is like a cube of pure white, but fingers of red light and shadow caress it. The darkness is merging into the dawn. The rays of light and electricity compete lazily. The daybreak is peeping through threadbare green curtains which do hang across greyish plastic-coated steel wires suspended between two bronzed hooks, the Alpha and the Omega, the Word and the deed which must follow. He squints around and finds his feet and glides around to discover a stained square of plastic, here is the switch, he clicks it off, the bulb extinguished, and so did his mind. He plunged into an ocean of crawling patterns that dissolve like mirrors of soft wax. Then located the switch, pushed the rectangle within what has become an oblong, but dawn awaits outside in the world.

In that place lurk purple serpents with green eyes composed of composite deceptions, ice that burns like Sulphur of hell. I had fled, knowing I am both ice and purgatory. My heart is both torn and crimson, yet it is not cold or black nor twisted but beats blood. I pick up a knife to defend myself from the serpents but then realise I had not slept

for many days and nights. There is no glint from the blade because the moon had imploded. Where is everyone? Noting dark red stains on my clothes, I just plunged the knife inwards. A siren as if from Ulysses' longest sentence tied ribbons of words around my body. Yes, it was Joyce and the twisted and winding sentence written in 1922, which had held 3,687 words. Cast upon rocks and wrecked yet bound with a tape measure of black and white, comments on cotton, ideas in heads, Beauty is Truth and that is all I need to know on Earth spoken by John Keats.
.

   Now I was happy to sleep.

On 'Spooks.'
A Petrarchan Sonnet.

You speak in heighten phraseology,
You had believed our fight soulless,
But never had avoided us on purpose,
A tape records a list of pharmacology.
We chat using only Leftist terminology,
We talk in words that are meaningless,
We wink again as they are senseless,
And then grimace at their eschatology.

Our Nemesis will tear down their dawn,
They are already marked in pens of red,
Then crawl into rabbit holes hidden down,
But will only bury those they put into bed,
Were lobotomised when in Portland Down,
Those zombies had served the living dead.

Two traditional Haiku.

01.

Summer has fragrant
Love with sweet scent, in moonlight
    We can only weep.

02.

Cherry blossom crowns
The lovers' summer, madman
Your blossom is hail.

A modern Haiku.

A haiku written in memory of Edie Sedgwick (1943-1971).

Bliss was fixing fire
In shadows, flower of flame
You wilted to bloom.

(Lines upon reading Charlotte Mew: 'Magdeleine in Church'*).

Our breath heavy, honeyed, tortured, and curved,
Shiny black boots were dark and gloss orbit in sin,
She was almost a stormtrooper when enraptured,
I rolled into a ball and hoped not to sing that hymn.
That whip was raised as if on 1936 Olympian day,
It cracked with whacks like goose-stepping troops,
Can they love like sheep who come on Sunday?
You and I, we know the meaning of our troupes.
Is sin delight Mary when Our Lady was so far
Away, only had drunk with sad and evil men,
So had laid in a gutter while we gazed at a star,
Then crawled to Mass, and read Nietzsche a madman.
If God was dead, all that remains is an absurd vocation,
For that ball and chain never gave her satisfaction.

*Charlotte Mew's poem, the longest she wrote @ 222 lines, Magdeleine in Church. The first printers refused to set it when published in her debut collection, The Farmer's Bride (1916). Julia Copus (2021), in her biography, provides two possible reasons. First, the printers may have been genuinely outraged on religious grounds or, more likely, because DH Lawrence's The Rainbow had been banned and publicly burned recently, they were frightened.

The Steppenwolf.

A wolf had wandered the Steppes in a dance of solitude that desert of snow had stretched endlessly; it glistened,
Those expanses had no horizon; rays burned his eyes
And burrowed into a heart woven of silk, this is the price
He paid for his emancipation, an escape into a wasteland.

Tracks left will soon melt, for he leaves no mark,
The only mark is the one that cuts into his heart,
 From which he knows there can be no escape.

Frosted wastelands seemed today both caustic and angry, that sanctuary has imploded into icicles that cut, little mercy,
The Steppenwolf sniffed the air; it was chill like the slap of cold,
Then sets steady yellow eyes on the precipice and hurls himself.

A shepherd who carried a shaft of poetry secured by goat skin,
He wandered across a fertile valley with the tribe it was a flock,
So stumbled upon the corpse of the Steppenwolf, man or wolf,
Then rummaged through the belongings to find a wad of poems.

To transcribe these documents for three days and nights,
The Steppenwolf was resurrected and then had a tomb,
  Comprised of words, scrawled notes, and manuscripts.

I am the lost child of Simone de Beauvoir
I was made for another planet altogether. I mistook the way.
— Simone de Beauvoir, The Woman Destroyed, 1969

An Icarus had flown in those currents that whirl around the disc of frenzy and Truth, You were mother half-crazed with that music of Beethoven which caressed minds, And where else could that Appassionata Sonata be played but bliss in our heavens, A wandering Aphrodite chained to a cruel cross, our love was crucified and bleeds, Neither of us was of this world, but we were made of the stuff dreams are shaped by.

We celebrated our love of poetry and philosophy, you Muse of past and the present, My wings had whipped up some tempest as contorted limbs towards Time terribly, Until no longer your butterfly heartbeat for me, but drowned in a sea of golden coins,

An ornate veil hid a petrified perfection, that brute had finally bought and formed you,

Mind melts and blood runs sour since there is no sacred milk to nourish,
I am an amphibian without wings, gliding, sliding across pages of waves and books,
Solitary creature shunned by a world,
Hermit in a watery wasteland of thesis and writing.

An itinerant poet and a lover celebrate Mass,

A shimmering of shadows is pulsating from his crown of lemon light,
this has encircled with rays the waves
Of matted hair, slowly this exorcism of disbelief begins,
he is stroking the gold bond of slavery from her finger,
a breeze is caressing the sands from a forlorn temple into the red tints of mortality, an electric shock shoots through their grid, he bows before her mass of black forest, genuflects like Adam before Eve's temptation, they dissolve into ascensions of dazzled love, she is smiling and elevates the Host before him, they feast.

A teenage political prisoner is detained on wards x and y during the 1970s

An older monk on a secure ward also talked of Tim Leary and Che so we colluded, The nurse without eyes just a film covered one presumed in purveyor of darker art, A poet wrote in metaphor not grasped by those who had embalmed patients' minds, Children are born in a bell-jar of discontent but do not worry doctor has the thorium, But the clientele spat sputum into cardboard spittoons not emptied but flung in rage, So we were hidden on wards with sycophants, faces like brick and mortar monotone, A nurse wanted patients to be aborted cherubs of heaven, some were like banshees, No one commented until the ritual burial of a demon because things are hot in a hell,
Just play bingo pleads Janus the therapist as he winks at some wincing nurses,
No take over the asylum and make it your campus howls that interned revolutionary, The patients rise-up like tigers but then the panzer squad prepare a chemicals cosh, As electro-convulsive therapy was had by all in the aftermath, the wires just buzzed.

Not forgotten were those whose deaths in Stammheim Prison left us with bitter taste, Bitter is the taste of lemon, lemon is yellow that will colour us if cancer strikes in liver, But red will be funeral shroud as jaundiced eyes never glazed by cowardice of heart.

Poem to lost love

An intellectual is someone whose mind watches itself.
I am happy to be both halves, the watcher and the watched.
- Albert Camus, Notebooks 1935-1951.

The worms are in her hair and creep like crazy symmetry of slurred syllogisms,
Her black and translucent pupils are the corridor back into the infinity of inferno,
The nymphets were left broken like alabaster dolls sacrificed to a dumb phallus, Some gathered their skirts and stole the microdots hidden in haste but now lost, Camus stands alone a pillar of stone and utters his words of wisdom but weeps, Back in Sputnik I spin trying to keep the letters of R. D. Laing's Knots on a page, Tumble into a purple zone through a rose garlanded window etched in her mind.

Put the harpsichord concertos on again please I love them much Hermes sighs,
The statue of Camus vaporized, Hermes levitated, and we went weaving waves.
I write these words about those days of dreams and wish my love not died in vain, We were children of ether who were not of this world, entombed within its bounds.

A lightbulb (prose-poem).

He sits in a luxurious sea of crimson cushions observing a solitary lightbulb.
It is suspended, like his mind, by a single cord. This is pulsating slightly, or so it seems; no, it is the bulb flickering. The room, it is like being in a cube of pure white, is caressed by fingers of light and shadow. The darkness is merging into the dawn which is peeping through green curtains, they are hung on steel wires suspended between two hooks, the Alpha and the Omega. He finds his feet and glides around the bulb to discover a yellowing square of plastic, here is the switch, he clicks it off, the bulb is extinguished and so is his mind, it's cast into an ocean of crawling patterns that dissolves into mirrors of soft wax. He locates the switch again, pushes the button on and the knowledge of electricity envelopes his awareness, but that dawn lurks outside, there is the world.

In that place lurk purple serpents with eyes composed of composite deceptions, ice which burns like the Sulphur of hell, flee knowing I am both ice and in this purgatory That torn and twisted red heart you see before is not cold or black, it beats too much.

trait of my dead mother

You were confined in this sorrow, standing quietly entrapped by a drama,
With ivy script slowly bound you, an actress performed before audiences,
until weeping,
Her tattered mask dissolved onto a stage of dust with whispers of infinity.
Our mime was like an ancient memory, a text with those tears that burnt.

 I light a candle; it flickers in this night of cobweb.

What a shame (In a physical health Medical Centre waiting room)

Ex-psyche nurse wanders in with an inane grin
like he is on gin says,
 'what a shame',

You are lucky your enamel is still in place for the
Herr Dentist had gouged out mine, Pull your own
daisy but you try that one again and any plastic
flower poetry is gone. Refresh memory on a ward
a decade past: 'you will never study philosophy', I
have. Whoops, the phlebotomist says they cannot
take that vial of blood you handed her, You clown
minus powder and paint; I am not insane say
some in Latin and Sanskrit, Poor nurse is absent
of mind and shame; is no more than a pain in a
patient's brain.

Mother, this is not not Maxim Gorky
Unlike Gorky the flower of proletarian authorial
voice,
this poem will not be like his novel Mother, It is
4.30 a.m. again;
and descent into Hades has begun because my
aged Eurydice is entrapped,
The Russian dolls within dolls within a mind must
be unscrewed, given autonomy, Orpheus and his
double Oedipus must descend and cross the river
of the Acheron,
a river of woe,
Gorky saw the year 1917 blossom, so
revolutionaries waited for the wind's howl,
the crisis came it was calm,

Mother is bewildered in Hades,
the proletariat is dazzled by reflections of commodities in mirrors,

Not writing Mother and no revolution is the Sisyphean burden for those expelled
from a heaven.
The ferryman, Charon, undying boatman charges each of us Orpheus and Oedipus
A fee: it is insanity,
The depths swirl in a twist of whirlpools which are typhoons of the mind navigated, Madness possesses these incarnations of Orpheus as children they were hurled out
into blizzards of acid,
Metamorphosis from Orpheus into Oedipus is ancient like gnawed wormed apple
bitten by a Serpent,
 The poet Ovid writes Orpheus abstains from love of women as things went badly
 'no',
The pen is numb and weary of the struggle with double demonization of the
mind and body,
Reality tears like shoals of piranha fish devour a pair of lovers,
I weep and the sea, the sea is crimson.

Poem for William Burroughs.

I saw the best minds of my generation destroyed by madness, starving hysterical naked, dragging themselves through the streets at dawn looking for a fix.
> - Allen Ginsberg, Howl, 1956.

Staring streets reflect the voids in your eyes
which are mirrors of the squares,
they exist without the pricking needle easing
chaos; you found the mainline again,
an embrace like an orgasm burning through a
vein, Zen with and without the hassle, this Light
strikes those chemical cells calling calmly to the
soul like the whispered welcome of nothingness,
The Absurdity is not in these oceans where
weeping tranquility tumbles into dreams for you
were dancing into the masquerades of non-being.
High womb-like peace sleeps, wake, write, weep,
fix again. You survived, died at 83 because being
you;

>   You always 'went first'.

Two traditional Haiku.
01
Sun is the fragrance
Of love breathe that sweet scent choke
And live in moonlight.

02
Cherry blossom burns
Bright for those it praises weep
We sleep in the frost.

Lines for Jed (down and out in London)
You, most precious saint of the sacrament from beyond enlightenment,
we had stalked along the pavements of dust that billowed into our minds,
Core like mine was pure Zen Void tied to the sacred vein in knots,
A dazed Dionysus with tongue of fire roaring love for our tribe,
Contempt for those swarms of ants that crawl in rhythmic conformity,
Squares within squares, pulsations of electrical energy
Who preyed on us, prayed for us blind to their encrusted corruption;
Beloved jive junkie whose crimson sedition is still shouting from misty eyes,
Down and up in London, still defying that recurring Obelisk of glinting black stone,
I hope…

The poet's tasks: a blessing or curse.
Still hard at heel, those steel bonds don't bind his mind like blinkers,
The fire is not to be quenched within his mind and body: a vocation?
Those flames which lick like lovers probing tongues cocoon, wrap Him,
But they just burn and erode the being, this is the poet's grained Fate,
No choice almost like a sort of pre-destination of despair, myopic mass.

Six Haiku

#1.
Rust burnt in a mind It was acid,
 now teardrops Explode euphoric.

 #2.
Corn stood strong golden
Ready for harvest, the rain
You brought left famine.

 #3.
 A heart was made of
Blue glass and beat
but it broke Smashed like smithereens.

 #4.
Madness exhales breath
To lift veils, there the sane gasp
For they have no air.

#5.
Vampire bat poets
Had sucked your veins, gave them blight
 The depths they needed.

#6.
 Love was spat out like Spittle,
 a flute is silent
For it has no reed.

The Blood-Jet

Poetry is like the blood-jet, it just keeps on flowing.
- Sylvia Plath, Kindness Collected Poems, 1981.
An Apple was offered by that delightful serpent,
she snakes into a syringe as the vein is hit,
Or gushes from the severed artery of a child when hit by shrapnel,
seeps from that cut wrist,
Her brilliance is in the ability to transform any piece of cloth
from pure white to a darkest red,
She flows through each every syllable this severed finger slides across tyranny of the blank page,
She is dripping from the poet's pen
in splendid crimson as from vampire's satiated mouth,
A poet's ink blood is deeper red being contaminated by crazy cells which is cancer, He had bitten the Apple offered, gorged upon it but it was not in the Garden of Eden but Hell, The Invisible Gardener had forgotten to give him entry to Eden, the poet fell before the Fall, Poetry is blood-jet, then anaemia leaves these poets prostrate before the death time wink.

Two classes, two poetics.
A hair and the width of it is all that matters on the scalp
because it is seething like greed,
You need trophies because of all those lost like any vulture searching for carrion, That bejewelled pen you posture with runs dry before any ink oozed to awake blunted nibs.

The nib of the masses is forged with both steel and blood,
it has the sound of thunderclap, It writes on papyrus, parchment and paper,
 the internet and is flexible like a willow in wind,
We have many pens, you know not all who hold them,
some scribes, sleepers and workers.

One History, two classes, two poetics and a single struggle:
        clash of revolution and reaction.

Poem of a redeemed suicide

An angel had fallen into Grace,
this is the damnation at the antechamber of despair,
Now beyond tepid temptations, he stumbles through the scrub of tangled blind stares Of unseeing eyes no, blind stares and jealous glares of those who claim to spare, This baptism is of sand, a font of dust just like those who are sieves, nothing there but Barbed wire and head holes, the fruitless bites of those rotten apples make me puke into an abyss which is home I know it well, here the lotus flower blossoms at 5.00 a.m. A poet was persecuted by the magicians of modernity the priest purveyors of psychiatry, His persuasions are portrayed in patterns of ink which we call words not smeared turds. Their wands are broken on a philosopher's stone which is were
the poets learn craft.

Her book of cold spells

Moonbeams awake again as the White Goddess
has crackled into his mind like electricity,
This morning the pen scribbles because a poet's
thighs are bound in tight bondage of blue,
A witch had locked the belt some barren desert
drifting time ago with her brass prison key,
She peddled tears and fears from a pious silence,
her book of charms only cast cold spells,
The bell had rung at birth to exorcise desire from
her body that perished in pure purgatory;
Curses were cast in her casket; she gouged out
hearts with a lunar-crazed cardiac surgery.

To tickle love again would not be my metaphor,
 But a rook woman who writes with dark thread.

The transformation

That saint of sanity is trapped in a glass menagerie of sanctimonious deceit,
Until a flea has penetrated the dome and flies around in search of dog dung,
The master of platitudes swipes the irritant into apparent oblivion with a fist,
 A metamorphosis occurs, and the black dot mutates into a fluttering bat; hideous Beauty is born. It crawls, leaving a trail of crimson slime on the floor.
Being blessed with a sound mind, the saint books a check-up with Doctor Sane,
The shrink, with a grin and a wink, says you have found your vocation Narcissus,
To be generous, I will diagnose you with schizophrenia, so you better play a role,
Go and roll into the foetal position because it is medication time says that the nurse, Insanity's martyr, lives in an asylum,
 but the shrine of Absurdity dwarfs it.

A latter-day leper

A bug was bagged just for moral sanctimony in a shop of a holy sacred music faith, It was a case of contagion danger so he is to be pillared as he must be on the fiddle. No nothing to do with appearance for they know not yes, they do he has the plague.

I have the flu so have this rather large of box of tissues I bought at Boots just now, We do not want any of that here they say in a jerked horror which is spattered out, A leper is not in a colony it is clear but is from an asylum, prison or infections unit.

They are so pleased until the parasite speaks and is sprinkling holy water on them, Exchange complete, money for folk, manna for Mammon, art thou holy hypocrite,
All are children of the bourgeois so germ smiles and says good-bye and they reply

This poet in amber begins to weep with ink these words for people cut like Knives.

Haiku.
The winter spirit
Smiles, mistletoe whispers but
Always breaks like ice.

Haiku
This sun shimmered stalks
 Of corn pieces wounded flesh
And shed icy blood.

The temple of Aphrodite
Shoot white light in a rush to entwine in pulsations with the ivy of death,
drown in that heaving tissue with our shadows of poetic nothingness,
we are cast into hollows
Here banshees awake us from frozen dreaminess with their folds of white silk,
they sooth our cries In temples where those melting molecules are vibrating, it is here that we weep with Aphrodite.

No more will the creatures of Prometheus fail in their tasks

A spark zigzags then you put a hand to cool the heat into this lake and your fingers, Became frost bitten and they just clawed us cruelly, the reaction we pose does not Require refrigeration rather a transformation from victims of timidity into blacksmiths Of molten metal, we fashion steel into objects of collective Nemesis, instruments of Retribution; Once buried and lost until the new vanguard of Spartacus performs acts, To lance a swollen abscess of pus, it must be drained, the bare-foot doctors Inflict A necessary pain an incision, a wound with History's scalpel, poets don't just wear
The masks of Dantesque masquerade, no; our dreadful dream is a relentless beam.

The chess board consists of 64 squares, are you one?

The chipped chess pieces, the pawns, chant their abhorrence at the Smooth and uninterrupted movement of both a Rook and the Queen, At the fatal power of the King's demise which terminates their game, He was checkmated because of impotence and ineptitude, you didn't Avoid being mated: the Grand Master who is reincarnated as a flea Studies the game, metamorphosis's himself into sticky brown slime, He then oozes onto the board, only godless like the inexorable tides, The tacky mucus seeps its way into the pristine checkered surface. Did you lead a checkered life or as cramped as the pawns, chipped and clipped, never raced from A8 to R8, only P-K4*, an anticipated Opening and so is everything else, just predictable like the ticking of A chess clock, you 'play by the rules', 'stay on the board'; secure, its Death-in-life because the brown snot is caustic, it will erode you until Deranged the only option is to plead for checkmate, you 64 squares.

The runaway
Darkness dawned as his swimming sperm and her
egg of shell fertilized in eclipsed dance, this was
genesis of the children who tumble in dust of
those goblins glared like death, They impaled
these children upon stakes of plastic prepared us
to become an adornment Of bourgeois taste that
square whitewashed prison-cell called family, It
begins as they as they hammer those first nails
into you the crucifixion Is by white noise, eyes
pierced by glass arrows until death comes aged
six, A body wrapped in a shroud of pins, The child
was resurrected at thirteen; he was beginning to
plough the lime furrow, through fields of lemon,
they had folded into a daze of hazy tangerine.
Conception in the desert
Jab a silver pin into any
Poet and see sand pours out,
 It flows into a scratched hourglass
Which leaks particles through dream's prism
Into desert,
here poetry is conceived.
With those relentless sandstorms, they are blind.

Elegy for Elise Cowen ('beat' poet: 1933-1962)
Your smile is bright with magic, it draws in verse,
To glimpse the 'straights', their vision is blurred,
And gazes inert, that form is carried in a hearse,
But you who danced the naked poetics preferred
The peace of wombs, the warmth, and 'rush'
induced seductress,
Our wastes are frozen with promises, caught and
chosen

This moth of candle and flame is burnt and wingless,

At dawn you're cupped in a wrinkled hand and have written
A lament of deserts and biting sand sings into the syringe,
Enchantment of the finite 'fix' less with accusations on pages scribed in blotted rings; this sacred insanity is vibrating your soul, a matrix
For jewels, the wind whispered opiate kiss,
it's In here where belief lies on the periphery, the poetry,

Ascends in grace with those from Auschwitz,
You stumble across the graveyards and weep in symmetry.

On poets who lose their sanity because of unrequited love
Love had sweetened tongues to caress in these dreams of bliss,
Numbed, this night is enclosed in a cell.
The shadows of desired,
Emptiness gaze from the melancholy in her eyes,
The poet is cursed by his plague of blindness.

Winter Haiku
Ice has formed across
A lone pool, words are crying
Beneath its smooth face.

Haiku on poets
Cut that mind of coils
And it bleeds an ink of joy
That is caught by stars.

Haiku No. 4
A pillar of stone
Has a cloak of golden
It wraps itself in.

A poet becomes catatonic

A heart of dust is fleeing the square of black onto white?
The silken veils are drifting into a river of mirrors,
here baptism is a transience trapped in a house of tears
With the Dead,
they kiss with burning words like bubbling acid,
which blisters until poetry is left mute.

Lines on the loss of love.

The poet had gazed into a sky of lime green clouds carved in crystal,
his mind Embraced a sun of white linen,
But her Sun sunk and spiralled before him into a World without those who love to roam the lunar scape; their poets fix into a dream,
that stratosphere is where the fallen angels who touch mind and body perform
 their undying ballet of love and lamentation.
The poet's moistened eyes can see only her drama of pain,
he genuflects before her bejewelled chalice,
but its wine has seeped into luminous gutters,
here the drunken poets tumble.

Metamorphosed

A crown of thorns is encircled by a ring of rose petals,
Its rays are piercing his eyes with confusion; she sits still
And listens to the foaming breath which winds around Her head like a black serpent; it is contracting; she is suffocating but pulls at the coils of this twisting snake and begins to heave and then breathes again, he pulls at the cord and drags
it down around his waist in silence,
He's waiting until the black-backed beetles have scuttled across their dappled floor; she now begins her chant, a Dirge to gods of dust and lace good-byes,
an exorcism of Insects, she is metamorphosing and flies out of a window.

Oedipus is expelled from Eden

Her tears of crystal are an unbound metaphor
dripping from those silent
 Pools of his mother's ocean of eyes, Oedipus
glances away, blinded with Pain, picks up a
Syringe and finds his mainline to tranquillity of
night
. In these depths there is a shadow dance of
desire and Oedipus is tied to the mast for this
voyage into a zero, Sirens, lovers, mothers and
the Madonna are the poetry, Their nectar is sweet
to taste, his tongue touches moist
Petals and caresses with the relish of finite
whispering.
But the Inquisitor gazes down, spewing us from an
Eden, we were beatified with a band of light
around our heads, but a bond of thorns is formed
which pierces
Both mother and son, so now roam an
interminable lunar wasteland.

Psalm to the poetry of joy

The moon rises like mist distilled from a burnt river to whirl with her humming until the bonds unravel, now she is caressing her smile into radiant morning, her dust is lingering it sprinkles onto dormant souls of night awaking our song of love to a golden dawn, the poet's pen is dipping into this chalice of nectar, we wander across pages with infinity and innocence a dance with the light and shadows of sacred ritual, Psalm of joy to a pristine moon and the drowsy sun.

The broken mirror (a journey into the subconscious of the poet)

Those eyes of a mistress at dawn cloaked in silence,
staring into the hollow vision of his sight like night, the poet,
 ancient like crazed Oedipus cast in marble,
burn with those licking flames melting these colours,

 Sucked into this still lake of mirrors,
 wind blows the butterflies in this star gazed flight,
 now we are ebbing into tactile darkness soothed by dusty lunar wondering.
The constant beating of hail shatters this mirror,
Frost-clad poetry swallows glass; we're stumbling Adams.

She is the bridge across the river of Death
A vulture sweeps on hidden currents seeking carrion.
We cuddled death and squeezed it out of a rock; the vibes began gliding around a hill of lush green grass overshadowed byA Gold Phallus.

The phallus ejaculated the words of the dull with a force that shot them high into the sky where glazed eyes are blind, drilled them into the side of the head where dilated pupils are gobbling madness into their depths and then a pink fish gulped their dirge.

Flying beyond the cruel clasp of fire and reaching the icy shady spheres where there was a river of sparkling glass which was fluid and flowed fast, a woman clothed with black robes approached, her face was deathly pale and her eyes dark and sad, she said: 'take my hand',
we floated on and skimmed across the surface of the river that sparks,
her whisper is melody: 'this is your end, dissolve atom by atom in my tunnel of night'.

Dreaming of the Muse.

On Poetry sweetest tears are wept,
Caressing the shadows of silence this Muse is ancient as Electra;
She whispers breath onto a tissue psyche, which vibrates like a web of gossamer: Dream with shifting sands like a vortex of voids.
Doves with broken wings who fly from a cage, scribe those poems of night which ache with love's sorrow.

Prometheus lives just outside of Babylon.

Echo
baby groover
Babylon dreamer,
drowsy demon fixing with Prometheus
bound in her silken lemon robe.

The writing of verse with night

The poet of night's desert begins to scribe like waves into an ocean
 whose mist is without dawn,
Drifting across these fields with wonder,
like the touch into swaying seas of corn and sun,
sigh with the lovers Like oceans,
their caress is dripping like wax and breath onto paper flowers,
swirling into an endless spiral of clouds.
Moonshine weeps into this ocean of nothingness,
 the dust is like a masquerade which is dissolving into white and zero,
Their masks melt, softening into visions like the oblivion
 with eyes shining, shadows like insomnia with dreaming.
 Spring's dancers wander across the virgin page with its sighing,
 this is a word beginning to form into a wave, a whisper of sand,
The cloaked pen weaves into this morning shimmer of cobwebs
 in which the Muse hangs suspended like eternity caught in ivy.

Poem without a title

No existence without language
 no journeys without those words to
Prepare self for this trip in imagination
A voyage deep below dive into the
Abyss that underworld it is here that
we write with our demons.

Two poets contemplate Salvador Dali: The Persistence of Memory

Her mind is opening like a lotus flower stung by a spear of steel,
her breath drifts in lemon Globules,
pupils are fixed on the door, which is woven from willow branches,
he opens an aperture to discover
A zone which interacts with her black eyes, leaden
By the mist of lunar storms,
they embrace,
bodies are like Cotton pages blown across a sea covered in silver scales,
until wrapped In a ball of silk, they exhale rhythmically with the pulse of the Earth,
the clock faces have melted.

To oblivion

That mistress with melancholia is sitting like a consumed
Buddha in my prison cell,
 Holy tears are wept dry here descending into a fathomless verse,
Feel the breath but never the caress of her soul,
Intimate with the finite of vacuums whispered like night.
The Inquisitor pierces this haven with voids melting our eyes of glass
 which are pristine with weeping, footprints in the sand are swept away in waves of
oblivion like spirals of hollow.

To Art.

The Void, its cloud has rain,
a spring to quench our sight,
to damn and pierce the pain,
But art is fire in flight.

Lines written in melancholy

Sweetest death you are the goddess of summer nectar,
The honey for the poet to drown in unconsciousness,
verse is prostrated before you, both in mind and body:
Holy One, Holy Oblivion, Holy Death.
We, the children of the soul's catacombs scribe our ink onto virgin paper,
The white page glances shyly, trembles a little, anticipating the pen,
A nib begins to weave tapestries of willow meaning,
these are cloaked in the shrouds of images floating along a stream,
we are wandering through this labyrinth of poetry.

Introduction to Experimental Poems No 1-6
Poetry, 'stream of consciousness' writing and
'Beat' culture spontaneity.

This introduction examines the historical and theoretical context in which Experimental Poems: No 1-6 were written. A method of writing which was developed with Freud's theory of the unconscious became known as 'stream of consciousness.' It was an attempt to penetrate the great subterranean ocean of the unconscious. This writing was characterised by an inner monologue which was: The direct introduction into the interior life of the character - Édouard Dujardin, Les Lauriers sont Coupés, 1887 Hence the reader would, by a free flow of language, gain access to the unconscious world. James Joyce and Virginia Woolf are examples of 20th century writers who combined 'stream of consciousness' techniques with realism. They wove complex patterns of language which were inspired, to a considerable extent, by Freud's discoveries regarding the nature of the psyche. The relationship between ego and id was of interest to those who would explore the mind for the raw material of literature. Like all 'stream of consciousness' writing, these poems are an attempt to 'tune in' to twilight areas of awareness which are inaccessible through conventional forms and, therefore, to illuminate the id, the unconscious. In an essay written by Allen Ginsberg, a 'Beat' poet entitled: 'Abstraction in Poetry' he suggests that the poet: Reduces the artistic medium to its essential properties - Allen

Ginsberg, Abstraction in Poetry, 1959 This could, he argued, be the poetry of 'pure sound' (Ginsberg, 1959) like some of the Dadaist poets. However, for Ginsberg, writers such as William S. Burroughs created an abstraction not merely of 'pure sound' but, also, with the energy of an 'altered state of awareness', the vibrant condition of 'pure mind' (Ginsberg, 1959). Their work exhibited the negation of a consciousness which is enslaved to the perceptions of the ego: The sensation of self-elimination of all being into the unconscious is the experience of pure poetry - Allen Ginsberg, Abstraction in Poetry, 1959 In his 1959 essay, mentioned above, Ginsberg describes William Burroughs' writing as: A noncommittal transcript into words of a succession of visual images passing in front of his mental eye - Allen Ginsberg, Abstraction in Poetry, 1959 However, the most significant aspect of writing, for the 'Beat' authors, was not their opiate induced dreaming, but the technique of spontaneous expression which was inspired by listening to improvised jazz: To sketch the flow that already exists intact in the mind - Jack Kerouac from Allen Ginsberg, Abstraction in Poetry, 1959 So, in conclusion, these poems are an attempt to transcend ego awareness and swim in a sea of unconsciousness by employing the techniques of experimental poetry to open the doors of perception.

Experimental poem: number 1
Caressed the echo of a void embrace's reverberation,
Ache descends in a river breaking the clasp of mind.
We are engulfed in this swimming of the id being tuned
for a birthing of primal mother,
She wept with the stroking of acid droplets
those have been caught in a leaking chalice.
These eyes are dissolved with a flickering of colours
 that is a still pool in the twilight.

Experimental poem: number 2
Poetry lives in a crystal teardrop,
It is here that worms burrow
 Spewing like the earth retching lava,
Clasped by the mind manacles slicing the body into daylight and the darkness,
night is whispering with her misty breath.

Experimental poem: number 3
Sand just flows through a honeycomb mind,
Ideas are blown across an iridescent wasteland dissolving into an ocean of beats, we throb,
a pulse with this blood wept in eyes cried for wandering poetry,
Descend int swarms of crawling echoes like the dissonant rhythm of chaos.

Experimental poem: number 4
Tied to a stake, this ravishing of fire
Caresses the free thought of the shrouded solitary mind,
Heretics burn in their emancipation, the purity of our conflagration
Caresses the cruel laughter of a celebrant who is mocking us,
we sing in the finitude of our damnation, visionaries,
we are incarcerated in the flames.

Experimental poem: number 5.
White light licks into an abyss with the touch of totality,
the tongue draws a kiss murmuring with redolence,
this is eternity with whispered dew, begin our sobbing like a dried lake, the butterfly is caught in morning flight wrapped in a veil, his temple of mediocrity,
she is beginning to scribe oceans of lemon, here night and its burning tears are coaxed into humming, the drowsiness is like twilight.

Experimental poem: number 6

The lunar chasm of verse free with association,
ivy acid dissolving the page into running plagues of caged rats,
wire trap-door is opening onto the desert as masks are cast in rivers of clay,
the smile of a bemused mystic at night,
she is writing with those caustic tears of fire to be entranced in the cloudy
 liquid of dreams, spike is eased into the mainline as infinity beckons.

She said: 'love is not enough'

Stole a ticket to her theatre
Danced with this ballerina of hurricanes.
 Dropped words into her bronze head
 That sparked, enflamed and revolutionised,
 Her nails dug into taut skin
 Leaving rivulets of tingling red liquid
Which flowed into my bamboo pen.
 I wrote lines of love welcoming Her lunar landscape,
Here we wandered
With Molotov cocktails primed and ready
For encounters with fascists or renegades.
But she became a reactionary, interrogating consciousness
, examining my arms like a drug-squad officer.
She said: 'You've got a needle-mark...a needle-mark from last night.'
 I replied: 'That was the only opportunity to visit my friends, the only chance to get away from your tight tangle. Yes, there is a needle-mark, we shoot bliss it's called white light white heat.' So, lost in wastelands of ice. Here is where poets and artists Freeze their colours into brittle webs Of nerves and then sever them. The tragedy.
is acted out we are tossed away on howls of orange wind into a welcome green trance.

'Mainlining' whilst meditating on a crucifix
Solitary the moon is weeping crystal,
Welcoming grey clouds which are a caress
 For her eyes glazed like glass spheres,

The dialogue is with silk veils like the nothingness which beckons death into twilight, we are tossed into whirls of dust.

He rolls up a shirtsleeve the needle marks are like stigmata, Brown and purple bruises that glare as shadows weep across the terrain of whispers. Glancing heavenwards our light is dancing into the voids of night, Silhouettes are roaming around this room, the Word is suspended on a cross of wood, emaciated bodies are sacrificed to this fire which is never to be quenched by the dew?

Lines on William Burroughs' concept of 'death-in-life'

Square hearts had stopped, they were
Just rusty bilge pumps, someone turned
 The switch off, what a turn-on
Never dug that scene with America
 And atom bombs, chant with those
 Of us who have a different sound and song to the
hooded-snake death dirge, breathe an autumn
wind of pure purgation, howl cathartic baby
burnout buzz madness. He had placed enigma in
caps. opened that cap, cooked it, fixed it, again,
again, hazy. DECONDITIONED HIMSELF FROM
STATE SUBLIMNIAL MIND MANIPULATION, He
had the sweet-death golden flight of Icarus, also
the endless labour of Sisyphus. Illusion, allusion
and delusion. Crimson crystals are burning
pulsating embers gobbling Inferno, is this a
solitary illusion like blood? stained sacred
Sacrament or an academic allusion to a sanitised
Dante, mistaken because

Although this may not scold your flesh forget us
Damned At your peril purgatory will not cleanse
you, Hell is where we weep wild like galloping
horses, just snorting this chaos, the delusion is
that heaven existed, no haven or home for us.

Speaking of viral poetry...
 Language is a virus from outer space...The author is simply a node on a network, through which ideas pass. - William Burroughs, The Ticket that Exploded, 1962.
 That fatigue can no longer frighten us like the ice sheets in the mind, it is beyond any vestige or manifestation of fear as glaring of sun drills eyes. The black petals begin to fold inwards when a gaze is or isn't fixed, tangles of twisted thorns of a tight thistle bush are forests of emptiness, viral poetry is written and formed into lakes of ice, from ice is refined the pure crystals that are polished into those old cold stars, they had imploded long ago creating the gulping black holes, babies' mouths who drink from a black nipple which oozes dark milk, it's ancient not nectar, it is the ingestion of the 'Other', us as dark subject, objectification is unmade. Promenaded people you wake up and don't think black holes are empty, scabby fingers are grasping the bourgeois hand and it shivers with revulsion, grey suited exorcists wail 'demon get out', but we existed for eons before Eden or logos; our word is an infectious virus. For you are totally helpless, we have convinced your best philosophers since Epicurus and inspired the poet Sappho, then lit the fuse around October 1917. We are the Virus made word, made material in your universe, we are Now cellular.

Some variations on a theme of unrequited love inspired by reading William Carlos Williams…

 a).
In autumn wind blew golden leaves like her sorrow.

b).
Have drowned in her lunar silhouette to wander in our shadow.

Summer of love (a villanelle)

Time melts: we thawed a frosty reality to dissolve ice with our love,
Our eyes whose dilated pupils could swallow any hardened gaze,
(You fell across this hallucinogenic Cosmos, these stars tumble).

We crucified the betrayal of damned love and stared to humble
That dark spark, we conceived this just like evaporating into haze,
Time melts; we thawed a frosty reality to dissolve ice with our love,

I touched with delicate fingers the clasp on your eyes to unbuckle
A stream, the purple fragrance of humming, a goddess was ablaze,
(You fell across this hallucinogenic Cosmos, these stars tumble).

You crumpled into a sphere of sighs encircled by white light,
 a dove whose wings were caressed as we dived into the sun in a daze,
Time melts; we thawed a frosty reality to dissolve ice with our love.

Our song was vibrating into weeping trees, nectar dripping, suckle
Each other's ancient milk which is a sacred libation with soft praise,

(You fell across this hallucinogenic Cosmos, these stars tumble).

Tangerine gasp intertwines in a frenzy of breath, it falls from above,
 Then we lie exhausted in a grave, our bodies consumed, but raised.
 Time melts; we thawed a frosty reality to dissolve ice with our love,
(You fell across this hallucinogenic Cosmos, these stars tumble).

The creation myth of Purusha in the Satapatha Brahmana (c.800BC)

Our minds may try and cancel, attempt to blank,
 this switch was flicked 800 B.C., he had over
1,000 eyes and heads,
 Purusha was total visual, complete sight, absolute
cognition: dived into night without oblivion. But a
core of zero he only became a number through
introspection, digging that nothingness until he
floats Around a crown of Lotus flowers, here he
discovered the warmth and softness which is Yoni,
he luxuriated 'I am.' But like poets at dawn without
a pen and paper he had only desire, he tore
himself with pure golden energy to Create 'Other',
lover, she became a daughter, they were black
and white flaming water and running fire: joined.
This act created you and you and me, so says this
myth. Ashamed, she ran like a gazelle fleeing a
lion; he would Become a gazelle; again and again,
he deceived her until they had produced every
animal on this Earth.

Your eyes are shining (a prose-poem)

Those eyes shine with emerald, green in our trip again, it has the certainty with which a frost in winter will freeze a blade of grass and is sure as a decaying autumn leaf of gold is trampled under the boots of eternity. But, my goddess of the lunar wailing, your perfume intoxicates the psyche of this poet as he is falling into a labyrinth of dreams. Here shadows are like obscured glass splinters which pierce the mind, we are cast into a fallibility of chained genes, they hang like globules of honey draped on a derelict hive. It is here we return step by step, through the honeycombs, past the corpses of dead worker bees to the queen who nestles her sterile eggs and beyond to the primordial swamp, there our stunted fingers clutch each other in a grasp of love. Your eyes are still as we come down again, so softly into our folds of tissue.

An incarnation of Sappho and her friend accidentally OD

Some spit with spite and call it love, but not us,
Not in a temple of Aphrodite, here Sappho tends A
flame which brushes her lips, they are burning
And red…now purple as the heroin hits hard like A
hammer thumping its heat up the arm into that
Galaxy of welcoming brain cells, the hypodermic
Hangs limp from her arm, I gently draw the spike
Out of the bruised vein, her arm flops diagonally
Across an orange cotton shirt, I clean the syringe
By rhythmically flushing water in and out and
Finally squirt the crimson juice into blue china
Bowl; next prepare my hit, we uncurl in a temple
Of Aphrodite which is where lovers can purr softly,
the floor opens like a gaping mouth and swallows.

Anne Sexton and her fellow confessional poets.
(a Shakespearian sonnet)
Her hands began to write a page with dew,
Those hearts had shed the haunts and bonds of light,
She turned and smiled to cast a spell, this guru
So tense until her pen began to write
A verse of storms, angels of night that share
 Her seas of lavender wept waves of wonder,
The sun had raised so red to kiss her hair,
She sat quite still and breathed like Buddha
 Her wine could sweeten bitter potions
But doctors, priests of modernity,
Were glaring flames, her poems were emotions
 They tossed to Hell with shocks of electricity,
This burnt into these hearts of love, the mind

Was numbed by barbiturate and lay blind.

Dreaming of Morpheus and William Burroughs (a Petrarchan sonnet)

 We groove along furrows to cut the wet pavement,
This street reflects an inner web, this glassy maze,
The path to oblivion, it melts like an echo of praise,
The temple begins to sing with awaking ferment,
The dream-powder, its magic is like night's scent,
A garden of delight where sight and tears are glazed,
 You spike the mainline again; this is not so crazed,
The cobweb is caught like a dream's finite content.
But Morpheus is a cruel god, in darkness confess
His bonds, we know his mellow, like a nocturne
We were naked, our mind's flow to be dissolved
A cloud whose rain which beats us nails,
Venus Always burns away my colours in eyes not taciturn,
What remains, the riddles of thought, never told?

A poet is sedated in a mental ward whilst contemplating death

Embrace lunar death of the most Holy beatitude,
You're swirling with particles of dust in winds,
Darkness has sung without light again like pacing seasons,
This lamb is sacrificed on an alter draped with staring eyes,
A chant of hollowness rises from the pulsating mass of communicants, Their empty eye sockets where love has been condemned By supplication, they genuflect and weep with tears of ice as the poet is prostrated
and given an injection of chlorpromazine.

A psychiatric nurse gets writer's block.

The nurse tightens as his bow bends back
to shoot arrows of poetry into folds of sky,
That vampire is sucking inspiration from us patients,
he falsely claims the tradition Of Dionysus as he roams the ward,
a giant glaring into our dormitory, we have hidden
Our words and pens in the secret place, here
We also store stocks of medication, kept just In
case of emergency, the tablet is stealthily licked
under the tongue, retrieved and then Hidden in a crack behind my
bed, the nurse's bow has snapped and his arrows fall upon us.

H.

H is for Hell,
H is for Heroin,
H is for Heaven,
H is for Helpless,
H is for Hopeless,
H is for Homeless,
Should have been aborted and lived in the safety of a bell jar
S is for Schizophrenia,
S is for Solitude,
S is for Suicide.
Fled fragrant suffocation in Eden for the bitter taste of brown sugar.

On glimpsing Gudrun Brangwyn in 2009.

An Aphrodite whose skin was smooth as alabaster hums along the pavement, daring V-back dress, she is hoping to meet her Dionysus who is embarked on the same sacred mission acted out each generation, tonight is Saturday night just like the last one. school is like mind freeze pressure from examinations pressure from the curriculum pressure from ambitious parents. Those minds are like tender plants, they need earth to grow but they are treated with pesticides, they are being maimed. It was the parents who were expelled from Eden and not the children, yet the children must roam a bone scattered desert. Aphrodite and Dionysus drop a few pills, gulp down some booze and dance their ballet of the senses...they hope she

'Comes on' next month. I caught a glimpse of Gudrun today
her eyes were fire yet ice and kissed the sun with full delight.

Abel gets paranoid. (a psychological study of Cain and Abel.)

Abel is trying to run but clinging dreams enfold His mind,
then caught without motion and maimed
By silver darts of fatigue, he sinks and screams out:

'No stop please': tumbling like a dice down a lime
Mountain he has lost those bleating sheep,
dazzled by eyes of glowing ruby which spit like
drops of a Bloody reverie, tears cling to his fingers
like Swords Of Yahweh, whimpers: 'Cain?',
who replies 'cool man, It's alright now I've killed
Dad; we are free as the birds'.

Blood and Water: the most ancient sacraments

 In oceans the waves can look choppy and boats seem tossed like flotsam,
 but dive deep down into the depths of these seas and there lurks a rushing current which can suck a person into a zero, drive you into insanity like a mob devours its victim who like themselves is a wept victim, vicissitudes cruel as the sea, so here in these black blind bloody depths are flows that can only be revealed by the poet; but psychiatrists claim a similar trade. Oedipus had loved his mother, this is the way of oceans, but when she was like a branch and snapped like her sea son, then damnation roared. Oedipus was never freed, love cannot ice, and the sea chains are ancient like tears and fears: tranquillity was new, not deeply grooved and a pyre was fanned like the prayers of St. John of the Cross, fire howled by wind It burnt Oedipus, so he returned to the familiar sea of zero where he lives as a shy amphibian,
there is no blood of Clytemnestra and Electra in this water.

Song to the oppressed: 'never trust men in suits'

A howl encrusted with sores and dressed in the persuasive vestments of
An abomination slips from those contracting grins, that is the priest enrobed In the cloak of an abortionist greets
the pleated wail of another cocktail party,
Another nightmare, so let them cruise in their seas of dollars and moral excrement, Beware you anachronisms because the lava of the oppressed is beginning to bubble,
We say: 'No shit you pigs, we're going to sweep away the dust from your theatre', You entombed bourgeois whose ballet of cardboard replicas is step, step, stepping To the toiling of a Death Bell, it is beginning to ring in their ears and they wince with Fear, our hammer, the mallet of History is striking their skulls only to reveal a vacuum,
Never trust that pinstriped suit smile; it's obscured with clouds and in terminal decay.

The cobra and the poet.

The cobra didn't wear a uniform, It slowly lifted a swollen neck which was ripened with venom, yellow Eyes darted and smiting tongue flickered, Jaundiced fangs impregnated a trembling troubadour With the poison of conformity, the poet felt nausea then stung revulsion: He roams across urban Steppes and lives with wolves to howl their words. A child recollects his mother's self-harm and then writes a poem The poetry of bonds had tightened around his throat, Those muscles which muzzle a heart were learnt in Blizzards of sharpened scalpels, her piercing ice, a child Had crawled into a ball so tight to forget the cut, it oozed Blood and burnt still warm into his head; her ruptured Drama would never cauterise, instead it pulsed with the Deism of a marauding herd of ghostly horses galloping Into a mire of black syrup, this had stuck and dripped in Globules from his crown of fake thorns which he threw Into the cauldron to brew with her tainted breath, they Inhale this scent until the pen

A child recollects his mother's self-harm and then writes a poem
The poetry of bonds had tightened around his throat,
 Those muscles which muzzle a heart were learnt in
 Blizzards of sharpened scalpels, her piercing ice, a child
Had crawled into a ball so tight to forget the cut,

it oozed Blood and burnt still warm into his head; her ruptured Drama would never cauterise, instead it pulsed with the Deism of a marauding herd of ghostly horses galloping Into a mire of black syrup, this had stuck and dripped in Globules from his crown of fake Thorns, which he threw Into the cauldron to brew with her tainted breath; they Inhale this scent until the pen writes in strokes of blood.

Hippie woman in a North London squat, 1973

A chick is sitting in silence within the broken shell of
An egg, her radiance ripples around the room sinking into
Beds I rose petals, now her gaze begins to penetrate the wall,
white light is flickering out of his hollow sockets of nil,
his murmurings are staring, but she moulds that lava surge Into a river.
She deflects energy into a collapsing circle; her breath is in lace.

Caliban is reincarnated as a snake.

A cobra lay dazed and coiled, with glassy fangs he injected
waves of electrification into molten blobs of wax, this serpent
was sliding Fin a fog of disinfectant around suburbia with hooded amber eyes,
they glow,
He hangs without the chains of slavery which burden that place, is poisoned by toxicity of blown innocence. We left the funeral in boxes, could only free ourselves from the cemetery of echo by escape
to LSD psychosis
to amphetamine dependency
to heroin addiction
to organise the proletariat
to advocate the armed struggle
to celebrate the sacraments of schizophrenia.
Poets wonder at love that blows like ribbons into infinity,
but write in cauldrons where the pure of Hades are floating.

Let us dissolve demons with poetry (lines for poets trapped in a ferment of the Inferno).

They pierced us with an ice thorn and claimed it was their crown of thorns,
No love, then write about it,
 Blisters of fatigue burn minds and bodies with their claws of phosphorus,
No love, then fright about it,
Comrades have been driven like cattle stumbling into the bloody abattoir,
 No love, then fight about it, Counter-culture dreams drifted into that deep and dark well of Narcissus,
 No love, then cry about it, cannot adore because serpentine cobra had spat into sad eyes and blinded,
No love, then die about it. Let us dissolve the mocking demons
WITH OUR POETRY NOW.

The day I realized René Descartes was wrong.
 You were an 'I' who could not pass through the eye of a needle too wealthy in ideas, That Doubt of dream games of molten wax, but you were not an explorer of Psyche, An ideologue who would never doubt Cogito Ergo Sum along his preordained Way, Conjured an Evil Genius to deceive all, the thought of deception without a hesitation, Squares become triangles in a Cartesian circle, round and round you were just dizzy, Baseline was always going to be Saint Anselm, the proof of perfection by God alone. René the rabbits were all in a bag the one you

pulled out was Carroll's White Rabbit, That day my doubt became an epiphany was when the lie of Cartesian Doubt died, An awaking of a lotus flower in the moonlight, rebirth in the mists of lunacy and love.

The broken mirror (a journey into the subconscious of the poet)

Those eyes of a mistress at dawn cloaked in silence,
staring into the hollow vision of his sight like night, the poet,
ancient like crazed Oedipus cast in marble,
burn with those licking flames melting these colours,
Sucked into this still lake of mirrors, wind blows the butterflies in this star gazed flight, now we are ebbing into tactile darkness soothed by dusty lunar wandering. This mirror is shattered by the incessant beating with hail,
Frost clad poetry swallows' glass, we're stumbling Adams.

Dreaming of the Muse

On Poetry sweetest tears are wept,
Caressing the shadows of silence this Muse is ancient as Electra;
She whispers breath onto a tissue psyche, which vibrates like a web of gossamer: Dream with shifting sands like a vortex of voids.

Doves with broken wings who fly from a cage, scribe those poems of night which ache with love's sorrow.

The writing of verse with night

The poet of night's desert begins to scribe like waves into an ocean whose mist is without dawn,
Drifting across these fields with wonder, like the touch into swaying seas of corn and sun, sigh with the lovers,
Like oceans, their caress is dripping like wax and breath onto paper flowers, swirling into an endless spiral of clouds.
Moonshine weeps into this ocean of nothingness, the dust is like a masquerade which is dissolving into white and zero,
Their masks melt, softening into visions like the oblivion with eyes shining, shadows like insomnia with dreaming.
Spring's dancers wander across the virgin page with its sighing, this is a word beginning to form into a wave, a whisper of sand,
The cloaked pen weaves into this morning shimmer of cobweb
s in which the Muse hangs suspended like eternity caught in ivy.

Poem without a title.

No existence without language no journeys without those words to
Prepare self for this trip in imagination
A voyage deep below dive into the
Abyss that underworld it is here that we write with our demons.

Lines written in melancholy

Sweetest death you are the goddess of summer nectar,
The honey for the poet to drown in unconsciousness,
verse is prostrated before you, both in mind and body:
Holy One, Holy Oblivion, Holy Death.
We, the children of the soul's catacombs scribe our ink onto virgin paper,
The white page glances shyly, trembles a little, anticipating the pen,
A nib begins to weave tapestries of willow meaning, these are cloaked in the shrouds of images floating along a stream, we are wandering through this labyrinth of poetry.

The spirit of Ulrike Meinhof addresses the bourgeoisie in 2009
Ulrike Meinhof 1934-1976

Our waves will wash away the sand into a sea,
Bourgeois fuckers your system is screwed Ripped off the poor and the tenants,
A hot and dry summer will scorch with fire and now burn baby burn.

Think you are stable... no just sinking into an ocean of Narcissism which is not pretty, never learn bourgeois,
Now your houses are being repossessed and the mind Twangs:
those robbed of their dreams awake you shake in your shoes as the ghettos buzz, start to tremble... you have failed and now the revolutionary Nemesis waits.
The Angry Brigade is aware and alert and the Red Army Faction has not forgotten, Socialist Patients' Collective flexes their minds and their trigger-fingers;
Do not think the Red Brigades are all banged-up inside.
Our waves will wash away the sand into a sea.

 Bourgeois fucker your system is screwed Ripped off the poor and the tenants,
A hot and dry summer will scorch with fire and now burn baby burn.

Storm and Desert
The fiery worms which burrowed into my mind,
Are like the maggots which are eating the soul,
Now they have died, drowned in a dark ocean,
 Which raged until evaporated by the biting sun?
That tempest has lulled and my thirst has abated.

MIND CLOCK
Integrating like the hands of a clock,
Pointing to the misty time of no hours,
Which passes its breath in the silence?
Slowly returning to the house of a self,
 Here are shifting sands, a wilderness,
And the clock has melted with a heat,
 Forget to tock in time with their Rhyme.

Morphine Love
A morphine angel stroked my mind,
As a mother rock her child to sleep,
And a lover touched the soft breast,
Like dew on the grass in mornings,
No chaos, just the gentlest whisper,
Love between sheets of dark death.

Heroin
I shot a dream up my aching arms,
 In a haze of mind just lost in a skull,
Calling names from my quivering lips,
Pastel shades soothed weeping eyes,
Heaven strolls like floating lilac lilies,
In that caressed pool of emptiness,
Forgetting the anguish of our hunger,
Go those thunderclaps in our minds,
We were at peace a dewy humming.

Gather the Fragments
Like a brown and ruddy crinkled autumn leaf
Blown, Swept by gales, tempests and storms,
While others gushed like the chilliest hurricane,
Demand you will experience equally the puss
Perpetually Like considering a mirror
This will crack with the intensity of stares.
 Who will gather those fragments?

It is alright babe

The needle pieces that loving vein,
Like Love smoothing a lover's hair,
The white-heat rushes up our arm,
 Into welcoming minds like sunrise.
Cruising with sleep forgotten eyes,
 I watched 'the Man' as he grinned,
He had shaken-up into the kitchen,
 Nobody else has clocked his move,
 I just rise and stumble gaining focus,
Walk with amphetamine confidence,
A crookery-high piled shooting room,
 Gently approach and smiling, saying,
'It's alright babe, give me that knife,
I have Valium in my pocket so relax,
Swallow four of them with water, relax.'
I groove back into the music room,
He finds my lost vein and another hit,
Tears have burnt farrows into my face,
 It was alright babe, because of Valium.

SHE

Woman is the manna on the breeze,
Woman is the wind that plays chimes,
The hands that play and stroke a harp,
They welcome like warmth, shy, sharp,
Respond with moonbeams on the lips,
The memories conjoined never separate,
 She is the stream entering green oceans.

She mutilates the temple of her body
My body has become a twisted shrine,
Is a tube of paste that is oozing slime?
 It must be cut to allow the pus to flow,
The knife straight blade purges wrath,
This is incense to be inhaled by them,
Intoxicate them like a cyanide pellet,
She, the ultimate soliloquist departs.

Today
The poets languish in the mental hospitals,
The criminals are running the government,
The poor live in concrete boxes or streets,
Mind-control priests celebrating the Mass,
We weep from bruised, blackened red eyes.

Before the incense was lit

Before they lit their choking Incense,
He was Dammed before the beginning of Time,
Fated to shed tears like autumn leaves,
Cursed to be blown by the hurricane,
Doomed to be drenched in raged rain,
Blighted at birth to be a series of selves.

A temple has been desecrated by fools,
Even before incense was burning scent,
 At the Farewell, let there be no lamentation.

Sleeplessness

Walking through these cold nights of bitter sleeplessness,
My being slid down the dust pipe, a Way of Nothingness,
 Images become distorted in a mirror of caustic Absurdity,
These are both within and without no escape they shout.
Will any kind of peace, wipe my clay body, feverish brow?
Will the whisky-bottle or the syringe be a cloth of comfort,
Just to hush, hush this chaos that burns like hell in mind,
 And dissolve the soul to stop the cancer eating my body.
This barrenness of spirit with the potency of emotions,
 They cut like a missed arrow of love pierces the heart,
 Lead to a desired death or a wilted bed of rose petals.

No walls, no floor

There were no walls of haven in a family,
And certainly, there was no heaven ceiling,
No solid earth floor to stand upon or walk,
It was sub-terrain world of misty shadow,
It would with certainty of sunset explode,
A fiendish and hellish land of like Inferno,
Where all were tormented by their demons,
A family where no family ever could coexist,
I was born no self, a Tabula rasa smashed.

On the scene
Look whose back on the Scene man,
Lay some dope on him, be cool man,
A little acid tunes him to the frequency,
Give some speed to wake-up a brain,
Do-him-up with smack to get a habit,
Look whose back on the Scene man,
O.D. Off the scene is blue he is dead.

One
That slimy silence is just deafening,
The Void, Pregnant with a meaning,
We, I, and all the People in my head, a
re mirrors of all potential Pathways,
through chaos and the atoms of self
, A social consciousness is just isolation,
Strangled by the honeysuckle of lover's
Woven nets, a betrayal of the revolution.

Two
A baby is weeping in a storm cloud,
 A prisoner on the rack is screaming,
 The parents rock to a belted climax
 Another baby born into The Inferno,
And the parents beat their breasts.

Three
 A tempest crested wave crashed on his shore,
Like the rhythms of the sea eroding a coastline,
Suddenly his body is flung up into a blazing sky,
Soaring with swallows on the wind's wild current,
Aware of the finite with the sea and its roof of sky,
Only to embrace the hummed Mass in his
cranium,
Police came and smashed, crashed down a door,
He, a swaying cornfield routed the thought-police,
To recruit them to the revolutionary proletariat aim,
 A sea is bashing his mind until free he flies away.

Five
I, like a chick who is emerging from an egg,
wanting not to be born,
 it has been ordained, In this farmyard with that choking dust blown,
 He, she, they are all pecking around for corn,
Just to survive to exist in this yard that is hard,
The farmer does not feed us chicks properly.

Farmers will not let these to live as they wish,
For this is the generation of the battery-hens.

Still yet a living frame without a soul,
 A fire ignited by the Earth's pulsations,
Lost youth travelled in a zigzag tonight,
 Still trapped in a maze yelling for help,
 A man is caught in the breeze, no farm,
Only the Owner within ploughs his field.

Eleven
The memories return in the asylum with breakdown trough,
 as when a woman lies with her newborn, no father to be seen,
I wander through fields of gold swaying corn and think of snow,
But Mozart stepped across the terrain of the self and the universe.

Inside my skull

Within the cave of one mind,
The skull of Dante's disciple,
 Roam two evil men, who shout,
They both accuse me of devilry,
One contorted group therapist,
 One a policeman with a baton,
They are stones within a soul,
They are beyond an exorcism.

Angie Baby

She has worn a blue wool dress besmirched with coffee stains
Buttressed against the cold and the World with jumpers and a belief in witchcraft. She hummed with delight and rose-coloured blushes when her breasts were caressed with holy lips of a prophet. Her heaven roamed across her flesh as his tongue darted and teeth nipped. Only to drown in a sea of esoteric sighs. I loved her with my soul, relished her body if not the mind, I had lost mine. We twinkled across the fields in the moonlight. Until consumed we lay and slept in reveries. The police found a poet in a graveyard one frosty night, he was insane and awaiting a Resurrection of the Dead.

For Sylvia Plath

I am resting in your grave of nettles,
Your purple soul weaves its entrance,
Like an enchanted violin it is played,
By the nectar breath of your mouth.
My living willow is in a sullen tomb,
It is alight with colour and matter,
It is animated by wandering sighs,
Flowing in a purple force, my blood.
So, you stroke like a lover, my pen,
 I write on pages midsummer frost.

An Elegy for Graham upon pondering W. H. Auden
        Musée des Beaux-Arts, 1938.

Ablaze this Icarus fell from the ticked time,
Auden missed the point in that 1938 rhyme,
I heard your voice aloud in the baying pack
Of mental nurses, they walk with a whack.

A cut of words was sharp and yelled aloud,
You spoke with Laing and chanted so proud,
We told of a world of flowers and revolution,
The staff still smear us; they have no solution.

Phone erupted, and anonymity croaked death,
A slip of the tongue, just Freudian foul breath,
Could be a trap set by those greened eyed,
My abbey echoed with words sighs it cried.

And death has dominion; it drinks with a thirst,
That silver chalice has wine which is our dust.

He remembered Elise Cowen and glanced three times at a lightbulb.

(A prose-poem.)
He sits in a sea of yellow custard cushions observing a solitary lightbulb. It is suspended, dangles like his mind, by a single withered cord. It is pulsating slightly, or so it seems; no, it is the bulb flickering. The room is like a cube of pure white, but fingers of red light and shadow caress it. The darkness is merging into the dawn. The rays of light and electricity compete lazily. The daybreak is peeping through threadbare green curtains which do hang across greyish plastic-coated steel wires suspended between two bronzed hooks, the Alpha and the Omega, the Word and the deed which must follow. He squints around and finds his feet and glides around to discover a stained square of plastic, here is the switch, he clicks it off, the bulb extinguished, and so did his mind. He plunged into an ocean of crawling patterns that dissolve like mirrors of soft wax. Then located the switch, pushed the rectangle within what has become an oblong, but dawn awaits outside in the world.

In that place lurk purple serpents with green eyes composed of composite deceptions, ice that burns like Sulphur of hell. I had fled, knowing I am both ice and purgatory. My heart is both torn and crimson, yet it is not cold or black nor twisted but beats blood. I pick up a knife to defend myself from the serpents but then realise I had not slept for many days and nights. There is no glint from the blade because the moon had imploded. Where is everyone? Noting dark red stains on my clothes, I just plunged the knife inwards. A siren as if from Ulysses' longest sentence tied ribbons of words around my body. Yes, it was Joyce and the twisted and winding sentence written in 1922, which had held 3,687 words. Cast upon rocks and wrecked yet bound with a tape measure of black and white, comments on cotton, ideas in heads, Beauty is Truth and that is all I need to know on Earth spoken by John Keats.

.

On 'Spooks.'

A Petrarchan Sonnet.
You speak in heighten phraseology,
You had believed our fight soulless,
But never had avoided us on purpose,
A tape records a list of pharmacology.
We chat using only Leftist terminology,
We talk in words that are meaningless,
We wink again as they are senseless,
And then grimace at their eschatology.

Our Nemesis will tear down their dawn,
They are already marked in pens of red,
Then crawl into rabbit holes hidden down,
But will only bury those they put into bed,
Were lobotomised when in Portland Down,
Those zombies had served the living dead.

The Sonnet was written by a latter-day Katherine Philips (1632-1664).
(author of Against Love).

Should I compare you to a statue of steel,
My sheep know this is a time of delusion,
At Mass, they fear to feast upon the meal,
We dry our sea of tears without an illusion.
That hum of minds was like a bloody buzz,
She was a wire on fire like a ghost on gas,
Our school of thought was not jiving jazz,
A man with radar that zoomed into cash.
His type is not for us because we fought,
Remained in banks like a painted clown,
He became green, the dollar was bought,
The tide has turned; we gazed and frown,
The God who reads these just finite lines,
I have a fear of Him as I know the signs.

To an anonymous woman poet met in 1941.

This woman is manna on the breeze,
And is the wind that plays my chimes,
The hands that play and stroke a harp,
You hold both an ancient quill and pen.

She welcomes with warmth, shy, sharp,
Responds with moonbeams on her lips,
But memory is like some tightened strap,
The heat of summer melts those buckles.

Fingernails dig into her temple of a body,
Mine just resembles your twisted shrine,
The pipes of lace are torn and ruptured,
The air begins seeping out, yellow fog.

We can only taste the creeping aroma,
But cyanide pellets crushed intoxicate,
She, my lunar soliloquist, has departed,
I choke on vapour, a last gasp grasped

For Elise Cowen (1933-1962), a Shakespearean Sonnet.

Your smile was bright like magic; it shines in verse,
You glimpsed the "straights", their vision is blurred
And gazed inert at forms now carried in a hearse,
But you who danced the naked poetics murmured
The peace of wombs, the warm rush seductress,
Our wastes were deserts without our promises,
Caught and chosen, a moth of delight, sadness,
That flame had burnt and had left you wingless,
At dawn, I cupped it, scattered it into the dew,
A hand that had written a lament in a desert,
Your mind is sacred insanity and subverted,
The sand sang into the syringe; it was blown,
It is here where we lie stillborn in that womb,
I stumble across graveyards wept in a tomb.

He glanced three times at a lightbulb.
(A prose-poem.)

He sits in a sea of yellow custard cushions observing a solitary lightbulb. It is suspended, dangles like his mind, by a single withered cord. It is pulsating slightly, or so it seems; no, it is the bulb flickering. The room is like a cube of pure white, but fingers of red light and shadow caress it. The darkness is merging into the dawn. The rays of light and electricity compete lazily. The daybreak is peeping through threadbare green curtains which do hang across greyish plastic-coated steel wires suspended between two bronzed hooks, the Alpha and the Omega, the Word and the deed which must follow. He squints around and finds his feet and glides around to discover a stained square of plastic, here is the switch, he clicks it off, the bulb extinguished, and so was mind. He plunged into an ocean of crawling patterns that dissolve like mirrors of soft wax. Then located the switch, pushed the rectangle within what has become an oblong, but dawn awaits outside in the world.

In that place lurk purple serpents with green eyes composed of composite deceptions, ice that burns like Sulphur of hell. I had fled, knowing I am both ice and purgatory. My heart is both torn and crimson, yet it is not cold or black nor twisted but beats blood. I pick up a knife to defend myself from the serpents but then realise I had not slept for many days and nights. There is no glint from the blade because the moon had imploded. Where is everyone? Noting dark red stains on my clothes,

I just plunged it inwards. A siren as if from Ulysses' longest sentence tied ribbons of words around my body. Yes, it was Joyce and the winding sentence from Molly Bloom's monologue in 1922, which held 3,687 words. Cast upon rocks and wrecked yet bound with a tape measure of black and white, comments on cotton, ideas in heads, Beauty is Truth, and that is all I need to know on Earth, words uttered by John Keats.

I was happy to sleep.

A Predator.

A tiger burnt cold as he circled a herd of zebra,
I await his next stitch as there is always a needle,
It starts with moves and little drinky poos for free,
But nothing is free with him, too long behind bars

Of pubs and prisons, a peppermint crème oozes,
Now he has charmed again 'have these Blues,'
His insurance policy whirled in one more oasis,
Why does he decide to deceive the stripy flocks?

Because he has nothing to fool within but a void,
Avoid I would if it were at all possible as it bores,
What of tribunes of the oppressed if not when?
A herd of zebra is dispensable not being lions.

I guess a 'crash-pad' is better than the streets.
    Shame about the zebra though.

But do you not blink at their gangrene gouged
               Limbs,
The ordered lines of stigmata upon stigmata, it

    All started with little drinky poos.

Two traditional Haiku.

01.

Summer has fragrant
Love with sweet scent, in moonlight
We can only weep.

02.

Cherry blossom crowns
The lovers' summer, madman
Your blossom is hail.

Prose-poem to 'tribunes of the people' when 'clean '.

"the tribune of the people...able to react to every manifestation of tyranny and oppression, no matter where it appears, no matter what stratum or class of the people it affects."
    V.I. Lenin, https://www.marxists.org/archive/lenin/works/1901/witbd/

The moon rises like mist distilled from a burnt river to whirl with her humming until the bonds unravel. Now she caresses her smile into the radiant morning; her dust is lingering; it sprinkles onto dormant souls of night, awaking our song of love to a golden dawn. The poet's pen is dipping into this chalice of Light we wander across pages with infinity and innocence. Dance with the Light and shadows of the sacred ritual. This is a Psalm of joy to a pristine moon and drowsy sun, you and I, humanity.

Yet we both know the multitudes remain in shackles, some of the iron, steel, or gold,
 not until tribunes of the oppressed have severed, sawn, cut every fetter can we rest.

A latter-day haiku on Stelazine.

Stelazine blue pill,
Knock them out no pain, life lost,
 Did anyone gain?

Lines on being under-Wordy: a 'found' poem.

"L=A=N=G=U=A=G=E",

a spontaneous overflow

She recollected in tranquillity.

A Pantoum on a 'hot shot.'

I woke with a web of words upon my face,
The night left a stain and taste of almond,
I wonder what this may mean; it was lace,
The taste was as bitter as a Norse legend.

The night left a stain and taste of almond,
She had suckled a word, the womb denied,
The taste was as bitter as a Norse legend,
They had come into my mind like cyanide.

She had suckled a word, the womb denied,
The birth pangs were like a tomb that lied,
They had come into my mind like cyanide,
I wrote with the holy writ, and then I died.

The birth pangs were like a tomb that lied,
She smiled, and I knew this was true grace,
I wrote with the holy writ, and then I died,
I woke with a web of words upon my face

Morpheus and William Burroughs (a Petrarchan sonnet.)

We groove along furrows to cut the wet pavement,
This street reflects an inner web, this glassy maze,
The path to oblivion, it melts like an echo of praise,
The temple begins to sing with an awaking ferment,
The dream-powder, its magic is like a night's scent,
A garden of delight where sight and tears are glazed,
You spike the mainline again; this is not so crazed,
The cobweb is caught like a dream's finite content.

But Morpheus is a cruel god, in darkness confess,
His bonds, we know his mellow, like a nocturne,
A cloud whose rain which beats us nails, Venus
What remains, the riddles of thought, always turn?
We were naked, but our minds had a flow congest,
This burnt away my colours in eyes now so taciturn.

William Burroughs speaks a dramatic monologue.

Those square hearts had stopped,
they were
Just rusty bilge pumps,
someone had turned
Their switch off, what a turn-on
We never dug that scene with America,
The atom bombs, we chant with those
Of us who had a different sound
and song
to the hooded-snake death dirge, breathe the
snowy
wind of pure purgation, howl cathartic
baby burnout buzz madness.

Allen placed the enigma in caps, opened that cap,
cooked it, fixed it, again, hazy.
DECONDITIONED OURSELVES FROM STATE
SUBLIMINAL MANIPULATION,
Unlike us, Allen, some did get clean but with their
floating purple cloud freedom.

We had a sweet-death golden flight of Icarus, the
perpetual labour of Sisyphus,

I was speaking of viral poetry: a prose poem.
Language is a virus from outer space. The author
is simply a node on a network, through which
ideas pass.
         - William Burroughs.

The Ticket that Exploded, 2014.

That fatigue can no longer frighten us like the ice sheets in mind; it is beyond any vestige or manifestation of fear as glaring of sun drills eyes. The black petals begin to fold inwards when a gaze is or is not fixed, tangles of twisted thorns of a tight thistle bush are forests of emptiness, viral poetry is written and formed into lakes of ice, from ice is refined the pure crystals that are polished into those old cold stars, they had imploded long ago creating the gulping black holes. Babies' mouths who drink from a nipple that oozes dark milk, it is ancient not nectar, the ingestion of the 'Other', us as a dark subject, objectification is unmade. Promenade people wake up and do not think black holes are empty. Our scabby fingers are grasping the bourgeois hand that shivers with revulsion, grey-suited exorcists wail 'demon get out, but we existed for aeons before Eden or logos; our word is an infectious virus. For you are helpless, we have convinced your best philosophers since Epicurus and inspired the poet Sappho, who lit the fuse around October 1917. We are the Virus made word, made material in your universe because our cells have penetrated. Fear smears; forget your tears.

A poem for William Burroughs.

Staring streets reflect the voids in your eyes
which are mirrors of the squares,
They exist without the pricking needle easing
chaos; you found the mainline again,
An embrace like an orgasm burning through a
vein, Zen with and without the hassle,
This Light strikes those chemical cells calling
calmly to the soul like that whispered
welcome of nothingness,
The Absurdity is not in these oceans where
weeping tranquillity tumbles into dreams, for you
were dancing into the masquerades of non-being.
High womb-like peace sleep, wake, write, weep,
fix again. You survived, died at 83 because being
you,
Of course, you always 'went first'.

Our Lady of Sorrows in Notting Hill Gate (1973)

That green-scaled goddess of grief how she is wailing from her brown soil grave,
It is here that the recently resurrected dead exchange their laughter without any lament,
But you, who are skeletal with yellow skin pulled tight in a smile of delight, you,
A beatified Courtesan who roams those connected on electrified tuned-in grids,
A heart wrapped in sackcloth, which is worn by those incipient lovers of chaos,
Here a frozen embryo begins to pulsate; it tastes, eats the bitter pulp of that
apple bit in the Garden of Pleasure,
Ice folds into our eyes until lost we are reborn into this spectrum of zoned silence,
I embrace you; you took the crucifixion from my eyes, and our eyes do bleed bliss.

A Sonnet (Shakespearean) for Anne Sexton.

Those hands began to write a page with dew,
Her heart had shed the haunts and bonds of Light,
She turned and smiled to cast a spell; this guru,
So tense until her pen began to write…
A verse of storms, angels of night who share,
Her seas of lavender wept waves of wonder,
The sun had raised so redly to kiss her hair,
She sat quite still and breathed like Buddha.
Her wine could sweeten bitter potions,
But doctors, the priests of modernity
 Are glaring flames; her poems were emotions,
They scorched them with shocks of electricity,
These burnt into her heart of love, your mind,
 A soul was numbed by barbiturate and lay blind.

For Elise Cowen (1933-1962), a Shakespearean Sonnet.

Your smile was bright like magic; it shines in verse,
You glimpsed the "straights", their vision is blurred
And gazed inert at forms now carried in a hearse,
But you who danced the naked poetics murmured
The peace of wombs, the warm rush seductress,
Our wastes were deserts without our promises,
Caught and chosen, a moth of delight, sadness,
That flame had burnt and had left you wingless,
At dawn, I cupped it, scattered it into the dew,
A hand that had written a lament in a desert,
Your mind is sacred insanity and subverted,
The sand sang into the syringe; it was blown,
It is here where we lie stillborn in that womb,
I stumble across graveyards wept in a tomb.

Greek partisans. [A villanelle].

The dawn awakes, we are cloaked in snow,
Snow melts to leave bare and bleak terrain,
My cloak is red, unlike that of a black crow.

This morning I know that knife will glow,
I shall shake with shame, with the stain,
The dawn awakes, we are cloaked in snow,

Some do not know the heaving lava below,
Or seasonal cruelty with the brutal agrarian,
My cloak is red, unlike that of a black crow.

A vocation of pain the shepherds do know,
We must herd the innocents to that asylum,
The dawn awakes, we are cloaked in snow,

No, do not bow to that ancient status quo,
An act of revolt she had been a partisan,
My cloak is red, unlike that of a black crow.

In Greek hills, our blood must always flow,
For Sappho, her struggle is in a golden gun,
The dawn awakes, we are cloaked in snow,
My cloak is red, unlike that of a black crow.

An Elegy for William and Dorothy Wordsworth when lost in Manhattan, 1998.

They walked bewildered in this storm,
That bled just like a dream of Thanatos,
And scream as if they were just reborn,
Are frozen in a reverie but Time is lost.

A face with sockets which had sad eyes,
She smiled a poetic Lucy as Wordy bent,
He looks for his ink words upon her thighs,
Lucy glared at his loved sister with intent.

She said 'you know he stole your words',
Wordy burnt hot was prepared to hammer,
Sister smiled 'but dear you smell of curds.'
Lucy pulled a blade, her words no stammer.

A third portrait of my dead mother.

You were confined in sorrow,
Quietly entrapped by a drama,
An ivy script slowly bound you,
The actress performed without
An audience, wept as her mask,
Had dissolved on a stage of dust,
A whisper of infinity it deafens us.

I was your only friend, we are alone,
The wolves are baying for our blood.

Random haiku.

Dazzling ray of light
Shines, the corn bends but breaks and
A lunar sea flows.

The stars set our course
 Black raven, but wild winter
Winds blow us apart.

The harvest is sown
Ad grown, the crop has ripened
Too soon and fruit rots.

Haiku for C'
 Sun beam sparkled gems In her hair,
the Summer burnt
Rivers until dry.

Summer Haiku.
 Until summer rain Fell,
my tears had nourished
Only fallow land.

Summer Haiku. #2.
Until summer rain
Wept only to nourish
This wilted flower.

ON M.A.D. (Revisited (Mutually Assured Destruction).

The dead have not yet dug themselves from graves,
The resurrection of wormed corpses had just failed,
 And yet struck by a shaft of moonlight I still awaited
Snow lay inches deep, a cloak of innocence clotted
Her blood which had drip, dripped from a blue heart.
It could be a sin to be confused when the Bomb fell,
Without doubt we had clarity our cloud of unknowing, MAD,
we had mutually assured destruction icicle cut, Gaia ached
in her birth pangs in these death agonies, I awaited

Her child amongst the moulded tombstones. That freeze
hardened as cold bit, but the Bomb fell, The coppers came
and crammed me in a plain van, Blurt 'where are you are
taking me', the hospital for Mad, bad and dangerous
revolutionaries was reply. 'I see' said the doctor, he turned
deep red not dead. Because just like the patient he was red
of marrow.

Two tribes, two poetics. (Revisited).

A wide margin on balance sheets is a joy?
On their blue lips it is just seething greed,
They need trophies because they are lost,
That bejewelled pen you posture with runs
Dry, there is no ink oozing from a blunt nib.
The nib used by the masses is forged steel,
It has a sound of thunderous bolts clapping,
It writes on papyrus, parchment and paper,
The internet is flexible like a willow in wind,
We have pens, scribes, sleepers, workers,
The masses are leopards poised to leap,
The prey better begin to click pray-beads.

In Memoriam.

The call beginning a week of flame from a purgatory,
Until a red button has been pushed a rare rant over,
A handset now sits safely in a plastic cradle answer
Machine, already it has reputed their frenzied story.
 An imp had spoken yet again to his Master jealousy,
I am the green-eyed monster but am well medicated,
To an extent not attained so it cannot be fabricated,
The wolf who howls but never learnt to have mercy.
My eye is drawn to the wooden knots in this desk,
A Third Eye sees his gnarled face contorted, sane,
The phone did not sleep, neither did a priest's pain,
I grab the phone, rock a cradle: 'you are just a pest.'
A head begins to whirl, and I see the pest emerge,
I swipe at this unwanted guest with its myriad eye,
Recovering I grab a swot, wallop until it does not fly
From a phone on a cradle on a desk await a surge.

An Elegy for Eleanor Marx. 1855 -1898

Tussy you are me and were the incarnation,
The heights and depths of seething workers,
A fatal flaw lay deep, a martyred immolation,
To live, to die, to fly and not be like a banker.
A Polish, Jewish, Irishwoman girl of the fight,
Organised the women and girls match strike,
Will Thorn who you taught to read and write,
Comrade of William Morris who did not fight.
You translated Ibsen for benighted masses,
And Madame Bovary with the dead Aveling,
He was death in life a cobra waiting for gas,
So strike he did a vampire sucked your sting.
That prussic acid and chloroform made dead,
Your blood has stained our flag a deeper red.

Illusion, allusion and delusion.

Crimson crystal reflecting burning embers,
Is this an illusion or an academic allusion
To Dante? sorry no we are in the inferno,
It may not exist for you but is reality to us.
 This hell is where we weep and are burnt,
The fire is almost beyond our endurance,
Here the horses gallop snorting red flame,
Your delusion maybe O.D. to find if it real.

Adam & Eve.

She is the breeze that carries a Spring scent,
She is a hurricane wrenching trees laid bare,
Her hand just strokes the poetic lyre with fire,
My lips wandered across her humming body.
Yet we can mourn the day flocked in Eden,
We engendered a species far to destructive,
Now that Paradise lies in tangled steel ruins,
Only the freedom of a funeral pyre can free.

A second portrait of my dead mother.

You were confined in sorrow,
Quietly entrapped by a drama,
An ivy script slowly bound you,
The actress performed without
An audience, weeping the mask,
Had dissolved on a stage of dust,
A whisper of infinity it deafens you.
 I was your only friend, we are alone,
Now wolves are baying for my blood.

in memoriam.

Many would not survive the medicines,
Our beauty was like the circling vulture,
A creature swirling above golden sands,
We had that look like the stoned idolater,
An outcast stumbling across a wasteland,
Now Stelazine is best said the ward sister.
It was just a ritual to cleanse misfits' carrion,
A corpse is pecked raw with hooded beaks,
Then we smile with toothless gums barren,
On Sunday's visitors come to visit us freaks.

Dylan and Caitlin Thomas drink themselves into oblivion.
Let us dance with our dream of death, g
Gasp tightly together, tumble in tunnels,
Chanting to nil, to cloaked zero, to chaos,
Until freed from this frenzy of whirling fire
We're stroked into sleep, a slumber of solitude.

The Ghosts of Icarus

The ghosts of Icarus are howling their haunting,
Rise like Lady Lazarus before the moon is bright,
Spectres delight in demanding a dreamy delirium,
They dance like rising dead, burrowing up eagerly
From their bejewelled tombs, my casket is cracked.
A doctor looks away in shame; he is not to blame,
The foe we fought cannot be bought by him or us,
We are the patients, addicts and prisoners in chains,
Bound, tight, chocking this entombment crushes me,
For the ghosts of Icarus are bellowing within a brain.

Death's wings open to embrace my mother in the fields of moonshine
Night closed her arms around your soul in a dance of stars,
That universe of vibrations is where my eyes sting with love,
You gave me the literature of dreams; there we learnt to hide,
We were stretched between the poles of our flows and ebbing.

Our hymn, a wilderness of fated roaming in search of crystal,
Wandering with tears that burnt those pleas touching colours,

An effusion of whispers surrounded by the drama of outsiders,
We walked through corn fields which were like a golden veil.
Rocked you to sleep, verse vibrating around a sea of lunar light,
Time has wrapped you in a melody, the meander of dreaminess.

Zero

I am
Not an ice cube to be thawed with therapy,
E.C.T, In my core poetry and love burns melted the tears,
They are weeping in that solitude where hailstorms,
The frost-bite consumes, it has devoured my heart.

When I introspect into many souls all I see is a zero,
Just the dilated pupils of their eyes and wastelands,
They see don't see anything when look a a solitary.

A Teacher.

Most human beings have just two eyes blinking,
Bertolt Brecht said: 'the Party has a thousand.'
She had a Third Eye, the Eye of a Buddha,
She spotted me hiding within lines of words,
Read my literature, saw something sparkle,
Gave Thomas, Lawrence, Camus, this feast,
I bloomed, petals opened to expose a writer,
Was out of place and time the school was not,
Sought nourishment in a wilderness of nettles.
"He is a rose who left in this desert will wilt", she
Warned and within a year acid melted my mind.

A Dr.

Bluestocking, blue steel, iron in the soul,
You put me in a locked adult ward at 14,
Back to adolescent unit merry-go-round,
Round and round adult wards correction,
One day you smiled I thought it was okay,
Most favoured lady, the disturbed teenager,
You explained the dark arts of your trade,
Two years in Hollymoor Hospital my home
. You crafted a book; it was the standard text,
The unit was renamed the Irwin Unit, I'd left,
I perused those lines of spite and contempt,
You must have hated some of us in reality,
The tears of blood run down burnt cheeks.

G.C.

An enigma in stagnation, embalmed,
A leaf that fell from the tree of death,
Were mute, was it all that Stelazine?
Or you'd gone to paradise or Hades.
Just vanished one day, media alert,
Wandered off, seized, no one knew,
They even dredged a local reservoir,
Not a puzzle solved, never forgotten.

Professor T.

You had a brand-new toy, the experimental unit,
You took interesting patients to examine carefully,
Manic depression was your 'thing', all types done,
 I absconded, injection when the police returned me.

Slowed, slower and slow down a dust pipe I went,
Lost interest in the hospital food, the Bread of Life,
On bed-rest twenty-four hour watch, this is torment,
You enforce my order, enforced E.C.T, wired me up.
Hurray, a cured patient to display to medical students,
We sat, their pens posed, I talked about Trotskyism,
They scribbled, you smiled and said 'back to the ward'.

Liz.

Dawn's death hung like a first kiss,
Dawn, she wore a wondrous shroud,
Woven from the honey of dew scent,
And her eyes echoed Time's echoing,
Like the chimes of a pendulum swaying.

She weaved a veil which obscured eyes,
Like November mist brushes countryside,
And spinning her thread from the Alpha,
She worked to the pulse of his red Earth.
For whom with her senses unbounded
Could awake at Dawn's deathly delight,
Or ignore the timing a spinning wheel,
Forget stroking shimmer of summer day.
But the thread she wove was awful, mortal,
Was this leaden Earthly sphere, she knew.

You were third time lucky, we buried you

In Praise of Katherine Mansfield.

All of those bourgeois women thought you were merely
A writer of cream tea fancies,
Something to be eaten and discussed in polite company,
To read without dark discord,
That is how your minimizer, a hated one who maimed words,
Your husband contrived a legacy, he would have succeeded,
But pristine manuscripts hoarded from the foe,
Your death had confounded all but the sisters of Antigone,
Bees who kept the wax,
Your honey was tainted by dark mind puerile man,
Not beloved of words,' bees hum
Bees sang manuscripts back
No censorious cancerous chocolate box sweetness.
Your stories were not howlers of slogans or Phallic thrusts like many in time of hope and hate, a weeper of words about woes of the world's women and the outcasts

Lesbian love, moonlight and the Aloe,
The white child runs away with aboriginals,
The police caught the child, thought police tried to catch you,
Love lightens corruption and your cry was one of 'Bliss',
An ascent Into the heavens where writers are in love with words.

He roams the catacombs at night with pen (2).
This dove with blood speckled on his beak
beckons you bewildered vultures,
He is carrion on which you gorge your appetite for
a feast of sacrificial writing,
The Lamb entombed in his mind with a pen and
ink some paper without body, Blessed is he
amongst the lepers for they do suffer, no matter
you can mutter,
Do you still worship all those hangings from that
Tree of death, I ate the Apple
And know that maggots are burrowing out of my
bulging eyes the sober Adam,
In gurgle of death a holy mother condemned both
of us, Lamb and Magdalene. Magdalene of illusion
sits bemused and raving in her residence of a mad
majesty,
I await death and scribe the words which echo
around the catacombs of outcasts.

Cast the first stone preaches the priest.

Bourgeois understand the hands we priests swayed in praise were knurled twisted like Bitter lemons floating in tumbler of vodka that was a draft of dark wine we drunk for you, Nails were dug into plastic statues of a Christ by deranged middle-aged Pontius Pilates, Not extracted by Magdalene or Hail Marys rushed off in a fever of rosary beads broken, Cracked idols laugh loud deafening the pious and friends who are the cursed damned. A stream of crystal nectar begins to trickle, gush a torrent like the necessity of History, No the masses were only dormant, resurrected by revolutionaries conducting lighting, A branding iron will burn a mark on the lily flesh of the dollar as Molotov cocktails blaze, Not ethereal but delightfully physical women and men cast your stones, dawn is yours, No judge but the vindication by humanity:
  'the ends justify the means', Utopia on Earth.

The paper Buddhists.

The spectre is surrounded by shadows with their daggers drawn so do not exorcize. Because of her you are made flesh like all hermaphrodites her hungry Host prepares our salvation, you dig the Beast? Your friends are on the mend man so why carry that sacrificial knife still unsheathed, stop this inquisition, you like writing and do some chanting but we are still almost daft drifting through webs of ideals not made of gossamer or metal structure of Mammon. Turn of the screw twist your blades. Chalices of wine were like blood poured in ampules transmogrified into some caustic Acid dripped mind, are you Holy Fool we may be beached on isles, mirrors reflecting into each other, it is not stained glass just shattered windowpanes. Paper Buddhists cannot be unfolded as they were crumpled before they were born…

The poet hails a new generation of iconoclasts. Stone stumps stand in disarray and spew their lies in twinkling twilight these figurines are just like an imaginary harvest of grain in fallow land, 999 if you call 000 it is 666 chiselled onto their foreheads sad demons impotent to resist the forces of these nights, they have no conscience And will be gathered in a granary where a blind stone-mansion grinds, resistance races through a poet's pen like his father's phallus, he had Celebrated that patricide in a ceremony of self-immolation which was

SUBLIMATED it became lines of snow drops on the child-poet's mind in the lunar light. But wounds of lambs will no longer be cleaned with the antiseptic swabs, today's cuts are being dressed-up in gauze to avoid cross contamination. Now those stone idols of yesterday crash, smashed by new generations of ICONOCLASTS.

Can you explain fascism by psychoanalysis NO!

Organize the workers' militias!
Those fascists are drunks lying in the gutter with their icy blue eyes blind to the stars, like the animated dead in a vacuous chill morning covered in last night's vomit, it congeals, reeks as Nazi's lie in their bath until the water becomes chill, awash with decay and scum, afraid to the pull plug in case a frantic rat leaps out. Poor people should ponder we are strong composing our own songs of solidarity, it's the petty-bourgeoisie12 warps those symphonies of primal pristine perfection. Electra is pitiable as she stumbles through the zone looking for another hit of warmth and death deforming and distorted for in the unconscious Pater did not genuflect before her thorn garlanded shrine, she has worn the crown of thorns and used it to maim herself, is she hypnotised Caucasian Kali incarnate: No! Can you explain a fascist by their nightmares? No we choose either Left or Right, the masses awake from sleep, no dream analysis now it's who controls streets? workers bound by a shadow may become fascists, don't reduce this to therapy, one is a mental malady, but the only red remedy for fascism is a workers' militia.

THE POEMS OF A SHEPHERD UPON WAKING ONE FROSTY MORNING.

Poem # 1. Sonnet 18 revisited: [A Shakespearean Sonnet.]

Should I compare you to a frame of steel?
My sheep just know the wind is confusion,
At Mass they fear to feast upon that meal,
We dry a sea of tears with illusion.
The hum of minds is such a bloody bolt,
He was a wire of fire, a ghostly Lukács,
One school of thought always was bought,
He had radar that zoomed into the cash.
Your type is not for us because of misfit,
The night is still the banks the painted clown,
Forgot and went into dollars, you twit,
The tide had turned; you did not cast a frown.
The God who read these finite lines,
I have a fear of Him; I know the signs.

Poem # 2 The Shepherdess: [A Villanelle].

We thawed a frosty reality to dissolve ice with love, time it will tell,
Our eyes, whose moistened pupils could swallow their hardened gaze,
 She soared across the tempestuous Cosmos, a star of dust it can swell.

We crucified any betrayal of damned love, refused the death knell,
That dark spark, we conceived this just like evaporating into a haze,
 We thawed a frosty reality to dissolve ice with love, time it will tell.

I touched with delicate fingers the clasp on your eyes, they had a spell,
A stream with the purple fragrance of humming, a goddess was ablaze,
She soared across the tempestuous Cosmos; a star of dust it can swell.

You crumpled into a sphere of sighs, of white light, a dove in hell,
Whose wings were cursed as we dived into the sun in joyful daze?
We thawed a frosty reality to dissolve ice with love, time it will tell.

Our song was vibrating into the tree which was weeping nectar's jell,
Sipped each other's ancient milk, a sacred libation of pristine praise,

She soared across the tempestuous Cosmos; a star of dust it can swell.

Tangerine, it intertwines in a frenzy of breath, struck a golden bell,
Then we lay exhausted in a grave, our bodies consumed and fazed,
We thawed a frosty reality to dissolve ice with love, time it will tell,
She soared across the tempestuous Cosmos, a star of dust it can swell.

Poem #3. The Shepherd contemplates writing upon waking: [A Pantoum].

I woke with a web of words upon my face,
The night left a stain and taste of almond,
I wonder what this may mean; it was lace,
The taste was as bitter as a Norse legend.

The night left a stain and taste of almond,
She had sucked a word, the womb denied,
The taste was as bitter as a Norse legend,
 They had come into my mind like cyanide.

 She had sucked a word, the womb denied,
The birth pangs were like a tomb that lied,
They had come into my mind like cyanide,
I wrote with the holy writ and then I died.

The birth pangs were like a tomb that lied,
She smiled and I knew this was true grace,
I wrote with the holy writ and then I died,
I woke with a web of words upon my face.

Poem #4 The shepherd ponders the Steppenwolf.
(A Petrarchan Sonnet.)

I write the Golden Mean of eight to five,
My job to keep my sheep in an order,
The sheep would rue a marauder,
My crook the pen by which I live,
The game is not to work between 8 and 5,
Those hours must keep the sheep inside,
A mist descends; it masks the bold boulder,
The stone is rolled by wolfish stockholder,
It shall not hit my sheep whom I drive to thrive.

The grey wolf roams across the steppe,
Alone yet proud he is the one they fear,
For wolves must eat the meat of sheep,
He wanders without a single misstep,
He has a coat of fur quite grey like Lear,
Although alert and quick, a slick sidestep.

Poem #5 The Shepherd remembers the Greek partisans. [A villanelle].

The dawn awakes; it is cloaked in snow,
This melts to leave a bare, a bleak terrain,
My cloak is of red unlike the black crow.

This morning I know a knife will glow,
I shall shake with shame, with the stain,
The sheep to the slaughter must go below.

They do not know that irresistible flow of seasonal cruelty,
 a brute the agrarian,
My cloak is of red unlike the black crow.

 A vocation of pain the shepherds know,
 Must herd innocents to the subterranean,
The sheep to the slaughter must go below.

No, not bow to that ancient status quo.
An act of revolt, he had been a partisan,
The dawn awakes, it is cloaked in snow.

 In Greek hills blood must always flow,
Sappho the struggle of Syriza must pen,
My cloak is red unlike the black crow,
The sheep to the slaughter must go below.

www.ingramcontent.com/pod-product-compliance
Ingram Content Group UK Ltd.
Pitfield, Milton Keynes, MK11 3LW, UK
UKHW041410180426
11947UKWH00007B/39